Best Practice in Corporate Governance

Best Practice in Corporate Governance

Building Reputation and Sustainable Success

ADRIAN DAVIES

Routledge
Taylor & Francis Group

LONDON AND NEW YORK

First published in paperback 2024

First published 2006 by Gower Publishing

4 Park Square, Milton Park, Abingdon, Oxon OX14 4RN
605 Third Avenue, New York, NY 10158

Routledge is an imprint of the Taylor & Francis Group, an informa business

First issued in hardback 2019

Publisher's Note
The publisher has gone to great lengths to ensure the quality of this reprint but points out that some imperfections in the original copies may be apparent.

British Library Cataloguing in Publication Data
Davies, Adrian.
  Best practice in corporate governance: building reputation and sustainable success / by Adrian Davies.
    p. cm.
  Includes bibliographical references and index.
  ISBN 978-0-566-08644-1
  1. Corporate governance. 2. Business ethics. 3. Industrial management--Moral and ethical aspects.
I. Title: Corporate governance. II. Title.

  HD2741.D378 2005
  658.4--dc22

                                                                    2005022754

Library of Congress Cataloging-in-Publication Data
Davies, Adrian.
  Best practice in corporate governance : building reputation and sustainable success / by Adrian Davies.
    p. cm.
  Includes bibliographical references.
  ISBN 978-0-566-08644-1
  1. Corporate governance. 2. Business ethics. 3. Industrial management--Moral and ethical aspects.
I. Title: Corporate governance. II. Title.

HD2741.D378 2005
658.4--dc22

                                                                    2005022754

ISBN 13: 978-0-566-08644-1 (hbk)
ISBN 13: 978-1-03-283766-6 (pbk)
ISBN 13: 978-1-315-56908-6 (ebk)

DOI: 10.4324/9781315569086

Typeset in 9 point Stone Serif by IML Typographers, Birkenhead, Merseyside

Contents

Foreword

Adrian Davies' latest work moves the corporate governance debate on from concept to action. He explains the progress which corporate governance has made in different countries round the world through the emergence of codes like the Combined Code in Britain and of regulations such as Sarbanes-Oxley in the United States. Yet no one can be complacent about the way in which, in general, companies are still directed and controlled. The book points to the gap between the formal acceptance of code recommendations and ensuring that they enter the mainstream thinking of a business at every level. As the author says, 'The processes to deliver compliance must be rigorous, capable of measurement and reach all parts of the organisation.'

The book provides a guide to the processes that are needed to ensure that compliance is delivered in ways which meet these tests. The tone has to be set from the top. Leadership, as Adrian Davies rightly emphasises, is the driving force behind governance. It is the board's responsibility to set the company's aims, to agree the strategy to achieve those aims and to lay down the standards of conduct which have to be met in their delivery. It is equally for the board to ensure that its corporate structure is geared to implementation of the requirements of good governance. The HR function has its role in implementation through training, mentoring and ensuring that corporate values are lived and not filed away in codes of conduct.

Boards also need to clarify their policies on corporate social responsibility, the importance of which is well brought out in the book. Boards are involved with their companies' stakeholders and that involvement needs to be managed like any other aspect of their businesses. Reputation is a valuable asset. It takes years to build, but can be dented by a single unwise action. This leads on to the role of those who invest in companies in helping to drive compliance down through the organisation.

The link between good governance and good performance is now sufficiently established for most institutional investors to take governance standards into account in making their investment decisions. The liabilities of pension funds, for example, are long term and so the interest of those managing them should be in the ability of the companies in which they invest to provide a consistent and sustainable stream of earnings over that kind of time span. In their dialogues with boards, they should therefore establish that governance standards are in place and implemented, which will encourage such long-term growth and the strategies to deliver it.

As the book makes clear, shareholder companies form a minority of the corporate universe, but it is they who make the running in terms of corporate governance and set the standards for companies as a whole. They are also the companies in which the savings of the public are largely invested and so raising their levels of corporate governance is of fundamental importance to society. The book finishes with some interesting thoughts on the future direction of corporate governance and on the degree to which present approaches to governance around the world are likely to converge.

The author's analysis of the present state of corporate governance and of how its implementation can be improved are illuminated by some fascinating and well-chosen case studies. *Best Practice in Corporate Governance* deserves to be studied by directors, managers, investors and all those with an interest in raising business standards.

Sir Adrian Cadbury

Acknowledgements

In writing *Best Practice in Corporate Governance* I sought help primarily from the architects of the movement, in particular Sir Adrian Cadbury. This book has been built on the foundations which these architects designed and has been focused on ensuring that their plans are brought to realisation. As a result my concern has been to research examples of successful implementation of the codes which have shaped the design of corporate governance, rather than to re-engage in the process of advocating its adoption.

I am grateful to Gower for their continued support and for their encouragement to seek out best practice in a field where only bad practice attracts attention. I have enjoyed my search for examples of successful implementation of corporate governance and am conscious that some of my champions may turn out to have 'feet of clay'. (In my last book I featured Equitable Life!) I am grateful to those whom I interviewed and who responded both fully and frankly; I am delighted that I was able to find good practice in so many different guises and some unexpected quarters. What unites all of my respondents is their deep commitment to corporate governance and realisation that their personal reputation is linked to sustaining it.

My book has been shaped by people other than those featured in case studies. I have had encouragement from Sir John Egan, Professor Bob Garratt, Professor Bernard Taylor, Mark Goyder and from colleagues in the Corporate Governance faculty at Bournemouth University, led by Professor Nick Grief. Sir Adrian Cadbury provides support when needed and Professor Bruce Lloyd keeps me alert by offering regular opportunities to review relevant new books. To all of them, to my wife Kerry who has turned scribble into useable text, and to friends and supporters too numerous to name, I offer my grateful thanks.

Introduction

Corruptisima republica plurimae leges (The more corrupt a republic, the more laws it has)

Tacitus

The quest for effective corporate governance is a task which resembles the search for the Holy Grail. The legend of the Holy Grail originated with the belief that Joseph of Arimathea had brought the cup used for the first Eucharist to Europe and that it would appear to those in a sufficient state of grace to behold it. The publication of *Perceval: The Story of the Grail* by Chrétien de Troyes in the twelfth century led to sustained interest in the search for the Holy Grail and in the ways of achieving the state of grace needed to find it.

The need for an improved state of grace in the conduct of business became evident in a series of corporate collapses in the 1970/80s (Rolls Royce, Leyland, and so on) and later scandals (BCCI, Polly Peck, British and Commonwealth, and so on). These events combined to undermine the myth of British managerial excellence and to belie the integrity of relationships within 'the City'. What little state of grace existed had dissipated into failure and mistrust.

Being the main focus for discontent, the Stock Exchange commissioned a study by Sir Adrian Cadbury and his committee into the financial aspects of corporate governance and establishing a process for improving control over them. The Cadbury Report and subsequent studies (the Greenbury Report on directors' remuneration, the Hampel Report consolidating Cadbury and Greenbury, the Turnbull Report on managing risk, the Smith Report on auditors and the Higgs Report on non-executive directors) have developed a matrix of codes of conduct to supplement the provisions of law, in particular the Companies Acts. As a result, quoted companies have greater scrutiny of their processes, largely in a bureaucratic 'box ticking' mode, but little has been done to change people's attitudes and company culture.

Failure to deal with the poor 'state of grace' within many companies has erupted in a series of major scandals of a new type. Companies such as Enron and WorldCom had well-established procedures for corporate governance but these were bypassed by determined executives who wished to pursue a personal agenda. Another US company, Adelphia, was controlled and manipulated by the Riges family and looted on a massive scale. Nor was this purely an American phenomenon; the Dutch company, Ahold, was severely damaged by false accounting and one of Italy's largest groups, Parmalat, has suffered from fraudulent misappropriation of funds on an epic scale. The common factor in all these scandals is abuse of power by executives.

In researching for, and writing, this book I have been conscious that the quest for effective corporate governance has barely begun. It feels almost as if we have been rearranging the deck chairs on the *Titanic* and that some awful disaster has been building up inexorably.

One form this disaster may have been taking is identified by Don Young and Pat Scott in their book *Having their Cake … How the City and Big Bosses are Consuming UK Business* (Kogan

Page, 2004). This is an exhaustive study of their thesis that company executives and City institutions have for many years been working a shared agenda against the interests of shareholders and other stakeholders in their companies. City institutions are seen to have been feeding ideas for mergers and acquisitions (and disposals to fund them) to executive directors who wish to appear to be managing actively (and wish to enrich themselves as a result). Acquisitions of UK companies increased from £20 billion in 1990 to £170 billion in 2000. In most cases the short-term beneficiaries were the shareholders of the companies sold, usually at a large premium, and the City institutions. Executive directors benefited in the longer term, from increased remuneration and share schemes, although some, such as Sir Christopher Gent of Vodafone, sought an immediate bonus for an expensive acquisition. Given the reducing tenure of executive directors this impatience is likely to increase. For the shareholders of the acquiring companies most of these acquisitions destroyed value, since many were over-priced and few executive directors were skilled at integrating them quickly and effectively into their group operations. A 1999 study by KPMG showed that over 50 per cent of acquisitions analysed had resulted in a destruction of shareholder value. Such destruction of shareholder value can severely damage companies, for example Marconi and Invensys, and may prove fatal as in the case of Dalgety.

Why is corporate governance failing to achieve a 'state of grace'? I believe that this is largely because it has failed to engage humankind, individually or collectively. Judgement and action are human qualities, not those of processes or procedures. Corporate governance has failed to change the mindset of most business people, and it has not changed their behaviours on a day-to-day basis: 'Ticking boxes is done once a year "for them" – it is not part of my daily way of working.'

This book is an attempt to identify and explore the human dimensions of corporate governance in order to harness individual and group behaviours to the achievement of effective governance. At present executives are rewarded for meeting measurable targets, with little or no concern about how such targets are met. Too often the targets are personal, and their achievement may cause friction with other people. Failing to achieve them is frequently not sanctioned – often failure is rewarded, leaving colleagues confused and demoralised. Corporate governance depends on trust and co-operation with others, yet too many businesses are run on a combination of greed and fear. 'Old Adam' is strong in all of us yet we must all co-operate to succeed in our ventures. Finding a sustainable balance between spirited individualism and fruitful co-operation is the heart of corporate governance – is it also its Holy Grail?

Organising for Effective Governance

1 *What is Corporate Governance? Why is it Important?*

An early definition of corporate governance may be found in the Cadbury Committee Report of December 1992: 'Corporate governance is the system by which companies are directed and controlled. Boards of directors are responsible for the governance of their companies. The shareholders' role in governance is to appoint the directors and the auditors and to satisfy themselves that the appropriate governance structure is in place.' Ten years later the Higgs Report had a different focus: 'Corporate governance provides an architecture of accountability – the structures and processes to ensure companies are managed in the interests of their owners.' An international view of corporate governance is provided by the OECD Report 'Corporate Governance' of April 1998: 'Corporate governance comprehends that structure of relationships and corresponding responsibilities among a core group consisting of shareholders, board members and managers designed to best foster the competitive performance required to achieve the corporation's primary objective.'

Corporate governance is a development of the concept of government, which has existed from the earliest days of social organisation and has evolved into the elaborate constitutions of many of today's nations. Governance principles and structures apply to organisations with varying degrees of complexity ranging from international bodies, such as the United Nations, through national, regional and local levels, down to small clubs and special interest groups. Most of these groups have rules which regulate their conduct of affairs and facilitate the settlement of disputes between members.

The governance of corporations began with the charters for early commercial voyages and enterprises, for example, the East India Company, and business partnerships followed by joint stock companies, limited liability companies and consortia, for example, between airlines. Over time the constitution of corporations became more detailed and complex, incorporating customs and practices which had grown up round the early basic charters. These customs and practices were also codified into company law (statutes and case law) so that corporate governance became multi-layered.

The early days of corporations were characterised by frequent frauds and scams, for example, the South Sea Bubble, and Victorian novels are full of corporate misdemeanours and lawsuits. The introduction of the limited liability company in 1856 led to a rapid increase in incorporation. The ability to trade shares on a stock exchange helped to boost the value of successful companies and to weed out failures.

Initially most limited liability companies had close links between their shareholders and their directors, many of whom were also shareholders. This link facilitated communication and the rights issues of shares needed to fund expansion. As companies grew they required more professional full-time management, initially appointed below board level (as in many US companies today) but later some professionals became executive directors. This was necessary to provide depth and continuity in directing the company, most of whose directors were part-time non-executives with a portfolio of other directorships and interests. A typical company in the early twentieth century would have a part-time chairman, often a nobleman or a person with City connections, and a managing director who was answerable to the board for controlling the company's business. Later it became usual to have a finance director, particularly when the company had a large number of institutional investors who required briefing on the company's financial performance in detail. A few other executive directors were appointed to reflect activities of prime importance such as sales, research, and manufacturing.

This model remained in balance for many years but came under pressure after World War II. The end of Empire (and Imperial Preference), the growing economic might of the USA and the resurgence of Germany and Japan, in particular, created competitive pressures to which British companies were not accustomed. Their shareholder profile had changed; there were proportionately fewer individual shareholders and the weight of institutional investors increased as pension funds were channelled into equities rather than bonds. Two groups of shareholder emerged, individual and institutional, and their power and influence diverged. Individual shareholders had become numerous but most had small stakes in the company and few had links to individual directors. Their contact with the company was limited to receiving an annual report, a dividend cheque and an invitation to the annual general meeting. Institutional shareholders were able to demand more regular and detailed briefing on the company's progress and prospects, and were in a position to time the sale of their stake in whole or in part, if they were not satisfied. Institutional shareholders are key players in the City and have close links to the investment banks, lawyers and accountants whose activities drive the City machine. Another group whose influence was becoming increasingly felt by companies was the news media; their agenda was to exploit weaknesses in company performance and to find negative stories about individual directors.

Why corporate governance became important

Corporate governance became important partly because the classic model of meeting shareholder expectations delivered declining relative results and also because the primacy of shareholders began to be challenged. Between 1900 and 2000 Britain's share of world GDP declined from some 25 per cent to 5.6 per cent. British companies were driven out of major markets, such as shipbuilding, vehicle manufacture, computers, investment banking, and so on, despite sustained efforts to concentrate in order to build critical mass. Britain saw its lead in innovating key new products lost to American and other competitors (in jet propulsion, body imaging, genetically modified crops, for instance). These setbacks were reinforced by a number of company disasters from the 1970s onwards, forcing the rescue of Rolls Royce, Jaguar and others, and latterly by several major scandals (BCCI, Maxwell, Polly Peck, Guinness, and so on). It seemed that British business was not only failing to compete globally but was also at risk of internal decay. Such a situation was not only damaging to the British economy; it represented a direct threat to the credibility of the City of London as a market for investors. As a result the Stock Exchange launched the Cadbury Inquiry into the financial aspects of corporate governance in 1990.

Developing the codes and revising company law

The Cadbury Inquiry began soon after the Companies Act of 1985. This was a major piece of legislation which consolidated all previous Companies Acts. For this reason, and to effect change in the practice of corporate governance by persuasion rather than force of law, the output of the Inquiry was a set of codes of behaviour, against which companies were expected to report annually to their shareholders. This procedure was followed for the output of all subsequent inquiries – the Greenbury Committee Report on directors' remuneration, the Hampel Report, which consolidated and replaced both the Cadbury and Greenbury Reports, the Turnbull Report on managing risk, the Smith Report on audit and the Higgs Report on non-executive directors.

Following the Hampel Report, directors are expected to 'comply or explain' rather than tick boxes. This has made reporting against the Combined Code (Hampel) and subsequent codes more flexible and specific to company circumstances. It also opens the door to 'spin and window-dressing' to present company practice in the most favourable light.

In parallel with the development of codes of behaviour, the movement for improving corporate governance has helped to drive a revision of company law, to be integrated into a new Companies Act. Consultations on the proposed Companies Bill began in March 1998 with a major consultation exercise, around 'The Strategic Framework' starting in February 1999. The purpose of the consultation was to modernise core company law (excluding the Insolvency Act and the regulation of financial services), recognising the European dimension, with 11 directives to date, the EC Treaty and the European Convention of Human Rights (now incorporated in UK law). This process has now completed its consultations and the Final Report of the Company Law Review Steering Group was submitted to the Secretary of State for Trade and Industry in June 2001. One of the key innovations will be the need to publish an Operations and Finance Report, 'to provide a discussion and analysis of the performance of the business and the main trends and factors underlying the results and financial position and likely to affect performance in the future, so as to enable users to assess the strategies adopted by the business and the potential for successfully achieving them' (Company Law Review). Work on drafting the new Companies Bill continues and it is now well past the original deadline for legislation for reasons which are not revealed.

Beyond the codes – alternative models

We have seen that the Cadbury Report was commissioned to explore the financial aspects of corporate governance, since the impact of failure and scandal on the City had been financial, primarily through loss in the value of shares. The Cadbury Code and its successors to date have continued to focus on financial outcomes, though Hampel and Higgs touch on some wider issues, for example, the need to involve stakeholders other than shareholders and the need to create more dynamic company boards.

One month after the issue of the Cadbury Report in January 1993, the RSA (The Royal Society for the encouragement of Arts, Manufactures and Commerce) began an inquiry into the form 'Tomorrow's Company' would take. The inquiry was sponsored by a wide range of British businesses, under the leadership of Sir Anthony Cleaver, Chairman of IBM UK. It involved a significant number of interviews with chairmen and chief executives, together with the development of selected case studies into the sources of business success, supported targetted research on competitiveness and board-room values from a wide range of sources. The inquiry was concluded in June 1995 and reported as follows:

- British companies would need to change radically to cope with global competition.
- The fundamental change needed was to identify and work with stakeholders in order to maintain a 'licence to operate' from society as a whole.
- Directors' duties needed to be redefined to support this 'inclusive approach'.
- People involved with companies would need to be included in this 'inclusive approach' in order to motivate them and maximise their contribution to the enterprise.
- The financial community would also need to be included in this process in order to maximise their support.
- Companies would need to build relationships with communities and government to underpin their 'licence to operate'.

These findings represent a much wider view of corporate governance than that taken in the Codes. No longer is the company responsible solely to shareholders but it now has to seek and maintain a 'licence to operate' from society as a whole. All stakeholders need to be identified and included in the considerations of the company, more as if they were family members rather than through arms-length legal contracts. The range of stakeholders was seen to be very wide, and such stakeholders were expected to contribute to the success of the enterprise, rather than exploit it.

It is perhaps significant that the new Companies Bill adopts the concept of responsibility to stakeholders, and the 'inclusion' approach needed to meet it. Legislation usually lags original thinking and best practice, it consolidates them and generalises them by which time most of the competitive advantage of distinctiveness has been lost. This book aims to focus on the areas of corporate governance which legislation has not reached or which may not be appropriate for legislation.

The stakeholders in corporate governance

Corporate governance is a system for optimising the contribution of a number of disparate parties to a purpose which they are persuaded to share. These disparate parties are often referred to as the 'stakeholders' in the enterprise, and their potential for support or damage to the enterprise may vary depending on circumstances. The interplay of these stakeholders is the theme of this book, but it is useful at this stage to introduce them and explore their potential roles. This list does not include uninvited stakeholders, such as the media or special interest groups.

SHAREHOLDERS

Shareholders have traditionally been the key stakeholder in companies. In earlier organisations they would have been partners, and the partnership model survives into modern times, largely in small businesses and the professions. The function shareholders and partners have in common is ownership of their organisation. In English law the rights of property have traditionally had precedence over most other rights, so that ownership of a company gives its shareholders pole position in the ranking of stakeholders.

For smaller companies share ownership may still be a matter of pride and involvement, but the owners of larger companies have changed since the early days of limited liability. The growing involvement and power of executives has tended to make owners into spectators rather than participants; this tendency has been compounded by the increasing involvement of institutions as shareholders. Institutions do not think or act as involved owners – they hold shares as an investment and buy and sell purely for financial gain. Shareholders in most large companies are less likely today to think as owners, most will be using the company as a stake in their own financial game – some will be using their shareholding to advance other causes, for example, NGOs seeking to subvert company policy through pressure.

Lack of involvement by shareholders has been a major contribution to problems of corporate governance. The activities of corporate raiders in the 1960s, especially in the USA, were facilitated by shareholders who had no sense of ownership and were eager to sell their shares, irrespective of any consequences for the company or other stakeholders, such as employees. Executive directors became too powerful in recent years and have been allowed to indulge in take-overs, most of which have destroyed shareholder value. Concern about excesses in rewards for poor performance have only recently led to any action by shareholders. It remains to be seen whether shareholders will become more active stakeholders in their companies.

THE BOARD OF DIRECTORS

Historically the board of directors has been the agent of shareholders to direct their company. In the past many directors were shareholders or representatives of shareholders, creating conflicts of interest with their prime duty of care to the company as a whole. Even today it is not unusual for directors to be appointed by major individual shareholders, so that this conflict remains a governance issue.

Earlier boards comprised solely non-executive directors, with company management delegated to a general manager and a small team of specialists. As business became more complex and decisions needed to be made more rapidly, some of the managers were appointed to the board, initially the managing director, then the finance director and sometimes a few specialists. UK boards tended to have more executive directors than those in the USA, where often the only executive director was the CEO, supported off-line by a full management team. In Germany, Holland and Austria a two-tier board structure was favoured, with a supervisory board of non-executive directors (with representatives of labour, banks, and so on) and an executive board of managers. In the USA company boards were for many years virtually 'out of the loop' in terms of controlling their company, so that real decisions were taken by managers. Recently a spate of scandals (Enron, World.Com, and so on) has drawn attention to the weakness of company boards and the need to increase their ability to exercise control.

One of the key issues in corporate governance is the working of the 'agency principle'. This is the doctrine that shareholders are the owners of their company and that company directors are solely agents to exercise the will of shareholders. Company law enshrines this doctrine, so that shareholders have limited liability but directors unlimited liability in respect of third parties if the company goes into liquidation. In recent years many company directors have been tempted to behave as if they were owners of the company, following a pattern of 'heroic leadership' established by iconic CEOs in the USA, for example, Jack Welch of GE. An extreme example of this behaviour is Jean-Marie Messier, formerly CEO of Vivendi

Universal, who expanded his company to the brink of disaster. In recent times directors' rewards have matched the over-vaulting ambition of the role models among their peers. Restraining abusive levels of remuneration is now a major issue; the Association of British Insurers reports that most of their challenges at AGMs (in 2004) have been related to directors' remuneration.

One of the key challenges for corporate governance is to rebalance the distribution of power between shareholders and company directors, so that the balance of power between all stakeholders can be calibrated to meet the needs of the company in the context of society as a whole.

CUSTOMERS

According to Peter Drucker, the sole purpose of business is to find a customer. Without a customer there can be no business, since there is no cash-flow to sustain it. It might be thought, therefore, that customers are the prime stakeholders in any enterprise, with shareholders providing capital to serve them. The capitalist system does not, however, exist to favour customers but to create wealth for all participants. As with all stakeholder issues, balance is the secret of sustainable success.

Company law considers customers solely in contractual terms, largely as potential debtors in a winding up, and other legal relationships are contractual. In a wider context, however, customers need to be considered as major stakeholders and their interests need to be a key focus of management attention. Most progressive companies seek to build sustainable relationships with customers ('customer relationship programmes') which underpin future sales. Once again a balance needs to be struck between the company's interests and that of customers. Where customers have the economic power to subordinate the interests of their suppliers, the relationship between them is difficult to sustain. Major supermarkets have now the economic power to drive supplier prices down to unrealistic levels – such customers can be the stakeholder from hell!

Customer relations can involve issues other than price. Many enlightened customers involve their suppliers in their planning processes, even in the design of future products. With increasingly complicated supply chains, this relationship needs to be linked through different stages to achieve customer satisfaction. This requires a higher level of trust than has traditionally existed between customers and suppliers, and greater mutual commitment.

EMPLOYEES

Before the marketing revolution which put customers in the forefront of managerial concern, employees were a prime focus for management. Organisations which are 'supply-side' focused, rather than demand-led, are concerned to emphasise the provision of goods and services rather than respond to customer needs. Today this orientation is typical of public bodies and it is no coincidence that employees are a major stakeholder in such organisations and that trades unions remain strong in the public sector. Outside the public sector, the growth of global competition has made the ideal of life-time employment unsustainable and companies in the private sector have repeatedly needed to 'downsize' their employment to meet cyclical and competitive shocks.

Employees remain stakeholders in their company, however, since the company needs their skills and experience and employees can use the company to develop and enrich their curriculum vitae. Companies are increasingly developing a core of key employees whom they aim to retain and to offer advancement, supported by part-time and temporary employees and a number of out-sourced operations at the periphery. It is likely that companies will have relatively fewer employees in the future, and rely on contractors for services which are not distinctive or at the core of their business.

SUPPLIERS

Some companies did not identify suppliers as stakeholders until recently. I advised a major corporation a few years ago and had difficulty in persuading them that suppliers needed to be included in their stakeholders' programme. Traditionally suppliers have been treated with some disdain – told what to do and bullied into lower prices and faster service. When companies realised that it was expensive to have a multiple supplier policy and that picking champions for each speciality and working with them led to better service and reducing prices, partnership became the new policy. This has brought suppliers into closer relationship with their customers and is of greater importance at times of rapid change and of increasingly extended supply chains.

As companies become leaner in order to compete against low-cost competition from China, India and other emergent countries, it is likely that they will increasingly rely on external contractors. When IBM downsized in the 1990s it spun off whole operations to trade with them at arms length. Employees became suppliers. In the increasingly complex and competitive world we face, relationships will change, yet those involved are still stakeholders. It is increasingly common for companies who are usually competitors to be partners in a specific project. Stakeholder relationships make tactical changes possible.

COMMUNITY

Apart from 'virtual' companies, all businesses exist in one or more communities, from which they draw employees and suppliers and in which their customers may operate. Even 'virtual' companies have 'communities of interest', which may be the core stakeholders but which may involve their families in a wider audience. Internet companies do not have local physical communities but they have a wide audience of website visitors and potential users.

Companies have become aware of the communities in which they are located only in recent years. Earlier, some companies built their own communities (Cadbury, Lever Bros, and so on) in order to ensure a contented and dedicated workforce, but the majority were content to minimise their relationship with communities and recruit individuals. The activity of businesses can have a large impact on communities – the contraction of the coal, steel and ship-building businesses has devastated many communities where they were the sole or main employer. Government assistance relieved many of the worst cases but companies were often seen as unsympathetic. Sometimes communities are damaged by disasters, such as oil spillages, and the response of companies is not always adequate in such cases. Even after 13 years there is no settlement of claims from local communities in Alaska arising from the Exxon Valdez disaster.

In recent years companies have begun to recognise that the support of local communities is essential for their ongoing success. Concern to help build stronger communities is manifest in Business in the Community (see Chapter 7) and The Prince's Trust. Major corporations have established programmes for 'corporate social responsibility' in which they provide financial and staff support for community projects. These programmes are often supplemented by activity to protect the environment. Major corporations, such as Shell, BP, BAE SYSTEMS, and so on, publish annual reports on their work on social and environmental issues, which are monitored by relevant special interest groups.

Companies need to relate to communities in all parts of the world in which they trade. This involves different cultures, languages and religions; it also involves them in issues such as corruption, child labour and exploitation which may affect their reputation, even through third parties, such as suppliers, unless they are constantly vigilant.

GOVERNMENT

The last of the stakeholder groups identified by 'Tomorrow's Company' is government. This includes government at all levels and in all countries in which the company operates. It may be argued that government is a regulator not a stakeholder. This approach ignores the opportunities for dialogue which can be found through a constructive approach to government and the need for government to consult companies about ways to develop their business (and thus employment and taxable profits). No business, even Microsoft, can afford to ignore government and it is government which provides much of the infrastructure and services needed to facilitate the growth of business.

Many companies have tended to deal with government through trade associations and key contacts, such as local MPs. Larger companies have recognised the need to be pro-active in their dealings with government and public bodies. To do so, most appoint a Director of Government Relations, or equivalent, who can identify the key contacts needed in the public services. Companies increasingly use lobbyists to press issues with government which are of importance to them. Lobbying through trade associations produces no competitive advantage!

Government is not an easy stakeholder to manage. It is larger than any company and has the full panoply of authority under the law to protect it. Government can pass laws which are damaging to groups of companies, for example, changing tax regulations, and can require companies to undertake tasks for it, such as collecting taxes. Government intrusion in companies' affairs seems likely to increase, as governments reach the limits of taxation and borrowing. Government is a very real stakeholder – it has the power to destroy your company.

The dimensions of corporate governance

There are a number of models of corporate governance, some of which are based on structures and processes (such as the codes developed out of the Cadbury Report and its successors) and others which are not rules based but relate to an interacting set of principles. The advantages and disadvantages of each approach will be discussed in Chapter 2. At this stage it may be useful to draw out the dimensions of the structure known as corporate governance.

We have seen that governance is a system by which organisations are governed. For complex organisations, such as national governments, the system is intricate in its detail but should be clear in its principles. Lord Nolan, who was commissioned by John Major in 1994 to examine the governance of all public bodies, instituted a progressive review of 'Standards in Public Life' which has examined government and public bodies from top to bottom and is now addressing related issues, such as election expenses. The Nolan Committee established at the onset of its work a set of 'Seven Principles of Public Life' to act as touchstones for its inquiry. These are:

- Selflessness – acting solely in the public interest.
- Integrity – avoiding obligations to third parties.
- Objectivity – making judgements solely on merit.
- Openness – explaining actions fully; restricting information only to protect the public interest.
- Honesty – declaring any private interests which may conflict with the public interest.
- Accountability – being open to any scrutiny appropriate to the office held.
- Leadership – setting an example in observing these Principles punctiliously.

Another set of principles established by the OECD in 1998 included:

- Fairness – protecting shareholder rights and ensuring contracts with resource providers are enforceable.
- Transparency – requiring timely disclosure of adequate information on corporate financial performance.
- Accountability – ensuring that management and shareholder interests are kept in alignment.
- Responsibility – ensuring corporate compliance with laws, regulations and society norms.

(The OECD Report stresses that regulations, however well enforced, are not sufficient to promote best practices. The search for best practice is the theme of this book.)

These sets of principles (and others which are mainly similar) do not themselves provide codes of practice, much less rules, for running organisations. Their main purpose is to influence personal conduct, hence group behaviours, in order to build trust. Trust is the basic currency of human intercourse; trust enables people to transact with each other at all levels, and allows transactions 'on credit' which facilitate new initiatives and future paybacks rather than deals settled 'on the nail'. Where trust is sufficiently strong there is less need for contracts and regulations – 'my handshake is my bond' becomes reality and transactions are accelerated.

How do these sets of principles relate to the codes? The codes occasionally refer to principles, but it is possible to descry principles within their wording. Relating these perceptions to the Nolan principles there is congruence with the exception of 'selflessness' and 'objectivity'. These exceptions illuminate in a flash the basic cultural differences between the public and private sectors! Whether these differences will be sustainable in an increasingly assertive society to which both are answerable must be open to conjecture.

The concept of 'fairness' in the OECD principles seems to be different from Nolan at first sight. In fact it parallels the 'selflessness' of Nolan, except that it protects the interest of shareholders rather than the public.

The eight key dimensions of corporate governance

It is useful at this stage to take a fresh look at the purpose of corporate governance and how that purpose can be achieved. The primary purpose of corporate governance is to ensure the survival and sustainable success of the organisation to be governed. This is also the primary duty of company directors in company law. In order to survive and prosper, any organisation needs to define its objectives and identify the groups and/or individuals who have a stake in achieving those objectives. This process begins to raise the issues which the regime of governance will need to address and control:

- What are the purposes of each of the stakeholders and how may they be reconciled with each other and those of the organisation?
- What are the roles and relative importance of different stakeholders within the organisation?
- How can the energies of all stakeholders be harnessed to the purpose of the organisation with minimal conflict and dissipation?
- How can the long-term purpose of the organisation be protected from short-term pressures? And so on.

These questions (and others) highlight the eight core dimensions of corporate governance:

- The identity of the organisation
- The purpose of the organisation
- Leadership
- The distribution of power within the organisation
- Inclusiveness and communication
- The pattern of accountability required
- The maximisation of effectiveness
- Ensuring sustainability.

1 *Identity*   We all need to know who we are. Organisations also need a defined and clear identity, partly to distinguish them from other organisations and partly to rally support (saluting the flag). Who we are is partly the image we project but essentially the set of values which defines us. The image will be the symbol of the organisation's personality – like Johnnie Walker for whisky or the Legal and General umbrella; this personality needs to develop character by being identified with, and consciously living, a defined set of values. Developing character is reflected in the building of a corporate brand which attracts loyalty and custom and becomes the reputation which has value as an intangible asset on the balance sheet.

2 *Purpose*   Having clarified 'who we are', the next question is 'what shall we do?'. Defining the purpose of an organisation is part of the process of developing character, by adding depth to personality. Purpose gives the sense of direction to an organisation which galvanises action. It also acts as the catalyst for co-operation – individuals sharing a purpose and working together – which can be very motivating. The early Crusaders were an example of such motivation (until failure and disillusionment occurred). War and crisis are catalysts for motivated co-operation; survival concentrates all minds on an immediate purpose. Without the stimulus of fear, corporate governance needs to build and sustain consensus round a shared purpose and persuade those involved to leave their personal objectives 'outside the door'.

3 *Leadership*   Leadership is the driving force behind corporate governance. It maintains a firm focus on purpose and enables those involved to set each other an example in working to achieve it. Leadership is not the sole prerogative of one person, or a self-selecting group; leadership may change depending on circumstances, for example, a technical specialist may lead in a situation where patents are crucial. In a crisis companies often bring in 'company doctors' to administer harsh medicine; after the crisis a different form of leadership is needed. Leadership depends fundamentally on trust. The followers have to trust the motives, skill and judgement of the leader and the leader has to trust his or her followers to deliver their support. In Chapter 3, the issue of leadership is addressed in considerable detail.

4 *Distributing power*   In a dictatorship all power is concentrated at the centre. Dictators do not trust anyone else to exercise power and their followers are obliged to pretend to trust them. Even today some organisations concentrate power at the centre, often because of family control or because of autocratic leadership. The concentration of power rarely succeeds beyond the medium term – even 'Napoleonic' leaders make mistakes, for example, Jean-Marie Messier, and all are mortal. In a complex modern business no single person can be all-knowing and omnipresent so that distributing power to allow results to be achieved is the only workable model.

The process of distributing power, accounting for its use and avoiding abuse, and surrendering it when appropriate, is at the heart of corporate governance. Power is not owned by any single individual (even a sole shareholder is beholden to other stakeholders) and its use needs to be carefully scrutinised. Power is of value only to advance interests; to be effective it usually requires co-operation. A recent book by Paul Seabright, *The Company of Strangers* (Princeton, 2004), shows the inner workings of co-operation, and the process of balancing calculation and reciprocity between parties in order to achieve it.

5 *Inclusiveness and communication*   'Openness' or 'transparency' is a principle shared by all governance codes and its effect on corporate performance can be very significant. Openness is the basis for building trust which is at the heart of any meaningful relationship. In the framework of corporate governance openness is expected in all relationships so that information is communicated freely unless there is a corporate (not personal) reason not to do so. This is the inverse of the working of the Official Secrets Act 1911 which has been abused by governments and civil servants for too long.

Openness is also reflected in the principle of 'inclusiveness' which was established by the Tomorrow's Company Report in 1995. This requires companies to identify all stake-holders in their affairs and to involve them in their working relationships. Inclusiveness widens the boundaries of any organisation, both improving its intelligence and under-standing of the wider world, and making it more accountable to society.

6 *The pattern of accountability required*   All governance codes require accountability and the grant of any authority needs to be balanced by accountability for its use. Accountability is more embedded in public life than in the private sector but repeated corporate scandals constantly remind the public of the failures in accountability which damage their pension plans. Shareholders have often been weak in holding company directors to account and auditors have not operated objectively. The new Companies Bill, the impact of the Higgs Report on the use of non-executive directors and the recommendations of the Smith

Report should all begin to improve accountability but only if there is a will to hold directors (and others in the governance system) to account and to be more rigorous in how they are rewarded.

7 *Maximising effectiveness*   Corporate governance is directed at the achievement of an agreed purpose. Part of its role is to ensure that corporate activities are focused on 'fitness for purpose', both to enhance outcomes and to avoid waste. Maximising the effectiveness of corporate activities is a key dimension of corporate governance, involving action to ensure customer quality, minimising waste and building a sustainable reputation. Action to improve efficiency by increasing productivity and ensuring value for money supports this work. One growing criticism of the expansion of corporate governance is that it is 'driving out enterprise' and forcing companies to delist from the Stock Exchange. This concern is expressed in an article in the *Financial Times* by Richard Lapthorne, Chairman of Cable and Wireless plc (24 November 2004).

8 *Ensuring sustainability*   Failures in corporate governance are often caused by actions to maximise short-term results. Enron's collapse was partly caused by the need to report ever increasing quarterly profits. Corporate governance needs to focus on achieving results which will be sustainable into the future. To do so means that the pace of growth can be maintained and that resources match the company's needs. The governance system needs also to ensure that incentives for performance support a sustainable pattern of growth, so that personal rewards do not mortgage the company's future.

The governance system needs to optimise all eight dimensions consistently and needs to be proof against external and internal shocks. The management of risk is crucial in this regard, and is addressed in Chapter 3.

Governance and ethics

Ethics are often confused with morals but a clear distinction may be drawn between them. Morals are guidelines for distinguishing between conduct which is right or wrong. Conduct which is wrong is not moral. Ethics help to distinguish between actions which are not immoral, and both of which are 'right', but each of which may have different outcomes. Ethics enable us to deal with dilemmas where choices have to be made which have different repercussions for the parties involved. Avoiding and resolving dilemmas is a key function of corporate governance, not least in balancing the demands for short-term action against the protection of longer-term interests.

Interest in ethics has grown considerably in recent years, due in large measure to the practical issues faced by individuals and particularly by businesses, in an increasingly complex world. Issues such as corruption, child labour, global warming, and environmental sustainability are faced by many businesses; other businesses, for example, tobacco and alcohol, have issues around the danger of using their products. This growing interest in ethical issues led to the foundation of the Institute of Business Ethics (IBE) in 1986 in order 'to emphasise the essentially ethical nature of wealth creation, to encourage the highest standards of behaviour by companies, to publicise the best ethical practices and to demonstrate that business ethics involve positive initiatives, as well as constraints'. The institute is a multi-faith organisation with charitable status and wide support from major British companies. A key tenet of the IBE is that 'goodness advances with a mixture of altruism and self-interest'.

The link between corporate governance and ethics is also important as a means of broadening corporate governance from a focus on processes to concern about individual and group behaviours. Behaviours are the means of demonstrating values, which are part of a company's identity (see 1 above). Many companies have espoused a set of values for some years, yet few have learned how to embed those values in their culture. The mismatch between values and behaviours is a basic issue for corporate governance, and will be addressed in further detail in Chapter 4.

For many years the role of ethics in business has not been seen as productive of economic gain. 'Good' companies have been admired but there has been no proof that they are more sustainably profitable than average businesses. A systematic approach to this issue is provided by Good Corporation (see Chapter 8). Some fund managers, for example, Friends Provident, have established 'stewardship' funds to encourage investment in environmentally friendly businesses. Others avoid investment in arms manufactures, tobacco companies, alcoholic drinks businesses, and so on. Recent research by IBE and Gerard International, an ethics consultancy, has shown that there is a demonstrable link between the results of companies and their ethical behaviour (www.ibe.org.uk). Another initiative has been the establishment by the *Financial Times* of the FTSE 4 Good Index, which tracks the performance of selected 'ethical' companies and that of its general indices. A new FTSE/ISS Index was launched in December 2004 which will attempt global coverage of companies in respect of their corporate governance rating and their operating performance. No clear pattern has yet emerged but this new index may begin to draw one out.

Balance of power

In reviewing the outlines of corporate governance and seeking to demonstrate its importance, it will have been seen how crucial is the balance of power, both within and outside an organisation, to its governance. Power is essential to achieve results yet, like electricity and other forms of physical power, it is dangerous unless properly controlled. The dictum of Lord Acton – 'Power tends to corrupt and absolute power corrupts absolutely' – is as applicable to business as to politics. The harnessing of power to an agreed purpose is the key process in corporate governance which drives the achievement of results. The exercise of power needs to be controlled, both to avoid excesses and to ensure it drives only the achievement of the agreed purpose.

The balance of power in any multilateral relationship depends, basically, on the relative strength of the parties involved. Large companies have greater economic strength than the smaller companies with which they deal. Where this economic strength is so great that it threatens the balance of society, governments intervene to restrain it, using, for example, competition legislation. In the early twentieth century American governments acted to break up monopolistic power exerted by the major 'trusts' in steel, oil and transport. More recently American and EU administrations have been struggling to restrain the monopolistic activities of Microsoft. At the level of a corporation the balance of power requires to be controlled both between different stakeholders and between different functions and their leaders. Often the balancing act needs to work across both dimensions simultaneously and may involve external agents, for example regulators.

The balance of power between stakeholders is conditioned both by economic strength and by law. Economic strength is most evident in the supplier to customer relationship, but may be seen in employee relations where trade unions are strong or very weak. At the margin, even economic strength may be constrained by the law. Legal considerations influence the balance of power mainly through contract, for example, for supply, of employment, and so on, or through statute, for example, the protection of employees under the Safety, Health and Welfare Act 1989. Power is also balanced through internal regulations, for example, only non-executive directors may sit on the Audit Committee, cheques require two signatures, and so on. This network of controls is designed to limit the discretion of any one person, or of any specific group of people, who may wish to exploit the rest of the stakeholders. In Chapter 2 we shall see how corporate governance works internally to diffuse power; in Chapter 4 we shall see its wider application.

Regulation

There are cycles in corporate governance as in many aspects of society. In an ideal world people trust each other and work to maintain trust. This process requires a balance of 'give and take' so that relationships are strong and people can find their natural role in society. If individuals are too subordinated to society it is possible for that society to be harnessed to the ambitions of manipulative leaders – leading to dictatorship and disaster. If individualism becomes too strong society breaks down and the resulting situation resembles the anarchy of the Wild West. In order to avoid extremes and allow the daily pattern of transactions needed to sustain society, a third party is needed. This is analogous to the referee in a football match and requires the same independence and knowledge of human nature. This third party is a regulator.

In the past, regulation was exercised by the dominant party in society, usually a monarch supported by a priestly clan. The vertical structure of society has now largely disappeared in modern democracies and different groups manoeuvre to secure and sustain advantage, usually by negotiation, sometimes by force as with strikes. As society has become more complex it has become more difficult to maintain the working harmony necessary to sustain it. Law has fulfilled that role, both by statute and common law. The speed of change in society has made it increasingly difficult for statute to match reality, and common law, being based on precedent, is increasingly struggling to provide up-to-date judgements. As a result there is increasing use of non-judicial processes, for example, arbitration and regulation in a number of forms.

Many forms of regulation have legal backing, either because they were created by statute, for example, regulators for privatised utilities, or because they are subject to a royal charter. In general the UK has fewer statutory regulators than most European countries and a preference for self-regulation persists. The Take-over Code and the Code of Advertising Practice have established a British model of regulation by code which has proved to be fairly resilient. Sir Adrian Cadbury sees the balance of advantage between statutory and non-statutory regulation as follows:

The advantages of non-statutory systems ... are normally their speed of judgement, their relatively low cost and their ability to deal with new issues as they arise, none of which are attributes of statutory systems. A further benefit of the voluntary approach is that it can promote compliance, not just with the letter of the law, but with the intention behind it, thus setting a higher standard. Statutory systems, on the other hand, have the advantages of relative certainty, enforceability and therefore of fairness, since their rules apply equally to all.

(*Corporate Governance and Chairmanship*, Oxford University Press, 2002)

During the 'Thatcher years' there was a clear move towards deregulation, with many old statutes and regulations repealed or set aside. The increase of terrorist activity and recent corporate scandals in the USA have started a move back towards greater regulation, with a diminution of trust and greater reliance on clear rules. Where governance is weak or unreliable, trust is diminished and regulation becomes more powerful.

2 Different Approaches to Corporate Governance. How Can Corporate Governance be Made to Work?

We have seen how corporate governance became a major issue in the UK, driven initially by concern to protect shareholders from mismanagement and fraud by directors, which led to a number of large corporate collapses. The underlying concern was to protect the City of London from potential loss of influence with major institutional investors and avoid the flight of capital out of the UK. Scandals and corporate failures were not unique to the UK. Excessive trading losses virtually destroyed Metallgesellschaft in 1993. Crédit Lyonnais was brought to the edge of bankruptcy by aggressive expansion in the 1990s. The USA had its 'savings and loans' scandals and 'junk bonds' fiasco at much the same time. As a result most developed economies began to take an interest in corporate governance from the early 1990s onwards. One of the most active protagonists in recent times has been the European Commission whose 2005 guidelines on corporate governance are seen by many as a threat to national regimes.

A rapid oversight of the international corporate governance scene offers the following picture:

USA

The pivot for corporate governance in the USA is the Securities and Exchange Commission (SEC). This body regulates securities markets in order to ensure protection for investors and orderly trading. To do so it also regulates stock exchanges, broker-dealers, investment advisers, mutual funds and public utility holding companies. The SEC derives its authority directly from Congress and is active in litigation in support of the laws and rules which Congress has passed. It is, however, interesting that it is Eliot Spitzer, Attorney General for New York State and other state attorneys who have been pursuing Citibank and other companies (most recently Marsh & McLennan) for misfeasance. US regulation is largely law-based whereas British regulation is driven by principles. The immediate reaction in the USA to the Enron scandal (and others) was the Sarbanes-Oxley Act which put regulation into a higher legal gear; the UK has reacted to problems of trust through the development of advisory codes.

Few company boards in the USA have any executive directors, apart from the chairman/chief executive (the roles are usually combined), so that the operating model is, in practical terms, not dissimilar from the European two-tier board. For many years American boards were largely ignored, since investors and media talked to executive managers about the business and board activities were largely ritualised.

Academics and business writers, such as Peter Drucker, analysed companies through their executives and operations, since the board was usually ill-informed and behind the pulse of the company. The weakness of US boards encouraged the activities of corporate raiders, for example, KKR and T Boon Pickens, and many companies were sold out by institutional investors who discounted future earnings for quick profits. These fiascos and the failure of boards to control executive managers, both in avoiding catastrophe (as at Enron) and in preventing exploitation (World Com, Tyco, and so on), has led to increased accountability, a search for more independent non-executive directors (Disney) and a growing concern about remuneration levels for executives. The excessive power of chairman/CEOs is also under challenge, and the roles are beginning to be divided, for example, following the recent Disney AGM. The latest report of Institutional Shareholder Services (ISS) shows a decline in re-appointment challenges and proxy fights, as campaigners focus on issues in bigger companies.

JAPAN

Following the 1945 defeat, Japanese *zaibatu* or industrial groups were broken up and industry was closely regulated by government. The old linkages were quietly restored over several years to create a new set of *keiratsu* or cross-holding relationships, often with a core from the old *zaibatsu* groups (Mitsui, Mitsubishi, and so on). The need for Japan to recover after the war led to close government direction of industry, with a focus on growth in exports and market share rather than profitability. Growth was funded by loans rather than equity and shareholders were not involved in companies (even AGMs were merely rituals) and dividends were paltry. Take-overs were unusual until recently and external take-overs, for example, by T Boon Pickens, usually failed. The control of Nissan by Renault is unusual since problems are usually settled 'within the family' in Japan.

Japanese boards are largely instruments for meeting the needs of employees. Few smaller companies have outside directors. Monks and Minow (*Corporate Governance*, p. 272) state: 'Almost 80 per cent of all Japanese companies have no outside board members and another 15 per cent have no more than two outside board members. A 1990 survey found that of 33 013 board members serving 1888 companies, 91.1 per cent were company men.' It will be seen that Japanese boards are frequently very large, mainly to accommodate the different factions in the company. Where outside directors are appointed they usually represent lending banks or key outside contractors to cement relationships. Retired civil servants often take executive jobs rather than a board position, as a reward for earlier support of the company. Despite their size, company boards do not usually have much influence on company operations; lenders frequently place observers in the accounts department to monitor the health of the company more closely. Company boards do not usually meet frequently and the company is normally managed by the president and his operating committee, where real power is exercised and decisions taken which are only 'rubber stamped' by the board.

FRANCE

Many major enterprises in France have until recently been controlled by government. Some private companies, for example, Lyonnaise des Eaux, Renault, and Michelin have a very high international profile, but most of these have relied on a solid base of French market support in order to go global. As in the case of Japan, the government has sought to direct industry to meet the strategic aims of the state. Likewise, elite cadres move freely between the public and private sectors during and after their career, facilitating a shared policy and 'French' solutions to problems, for example, the exclusion of Novartis from the integration of Sanofi-Synthélabo and Aventis. France has a problem with its system of 'pantouflage' whereby the limited number of elite cadres from the 'grandes écoles' are placed in board appointments, often with government awareness. This has resulted in individuals holding large numbers of appointments, with conflicts of interest and limited understanding of each. The Viénot Report challenged the excessive cross-holdings and consequent cross-directorships and introduced ideas, for example, audit, remuneration and appointment committees of the board which echo the Cadbury Report. These proposals have subsequently been consolidated with the Report of the French Management Accounting Association (AFG – ASFFI) which acts as a working code of practice.

Most French companies are incorporated as a *société à responsabilité limitée* (SARL) and are managed by a *gérant* or general manager, answerable to shareholders. Larger and quoted companies are incorporated as a *société anonyme* (SA), led by a *président directeur général* (chairman/chief executive) who has virtually absolute power. The AFG-ASFFI code recommends that the roles of chairman and CEO should be separated and this is beginning to happen in quoted companies. The code also recommends that one third of directors should be 'independent', that is, with no conflict of interest. It also endorses the Viénot recommendation for standing committees of the board, on which only independent directors should sit. Disclosure of directors' compensation in detail is recommended. The code also sets tighter limits than French law on directors' terms (four, not six, years maximum) and age (one third over 65 not over 70).

GERMANY

Like France, Germany has a preponderance of private limited companies, *Gesellschaft mit beschränkter Haftung* (GMBH), over public limited companies, *Aktiengesellschaft* (AG). All companies with over 500 employees must have a supervisory board (*Aufsichtsrat*) as well as a management board (*Vorstand*). This structure has been adapted since 1949 to allow for employee representation on the Supervisory Board (up to 50 per cent in larger companies) and it already accommodates banks and other providers of funding. Exceptionally other stakeholders may have a seat, for example, the government of Lower Saxony (a major shareholder) has a representative on the supervisory board of Volkswagen AG. Germany has fewer than 700 quoted companies compared with nearly 3000 in the UK, where nearly 70 per cent of shares are held by institutions. In Germany nearly 60 per cent of shares are held by other companies, banks, insurance companies and government, and are traded less frequently. For many years the core of German industry has been the 'Mittelstand', privately owned companies (often family controlled) which have built up a substantial business in overseas markets. Most of these companies have been a 'closed book' for corporate governance purposes until fairly recently.

German corporate governance is rooted in the OECD principles of May 1999, which were codified for quoted companies in January 2000 by the German Panel on Corporate Governance. An official code was issued in 2002 by the German Government Commission, incorporating the work of the Panel. It deals for the first time with equality of rights between shareholders and has begun a move to dismantle the weighted voting rights which have hampered minority shareholders. It also forbids conflicts of interest between members of both boards and their duty to the company. The roles of both boards are clarified: 'The task of the Supervisory Board is to advise regularly and supervise the Management Board in the management of the enterprise. It must be involved in decisions of fundamental importance to the enterprise ... the Management Board is responsible for independently managing the enterprise. In doing so, it is obliged to act in the enterprise's best interests and undertakes to increase the sustainable value of the enterprise.' The presence of employee (union) representatives on the supervisory board has inhibited co-operation with the management board in many companies, especially where operations are moved overseas to reduce costs. Many companies have meetings of the supervisory board infrequently and limit its agenda to non-contentious issues. This conflicts with the new code and it remains to be seen how these conflicts can be reconciled.

THE NETHERLANDS

The Dutch model of corporate governance is basically similar to that of Germany. In 1997 the 'Peters Committee' established a code whose use is wholly voluntary. Concerns about transparency and accountability have led to an initiative to give regulatory force to the code, so far without conclusion. The Netherlands is also the home of several multi-national companies. Some, like Shell, Unilever and Reed Elsevier, have a separate quoted company both in Holland and the UK which is managed to local norms and their overall business is integrated through a management committee. Others are incorporated in the UK and are quoted on both stock exchanges, for example, Corus, which has a subsidiary in the Netherlands, managed according to local laws. Shell has adopted a similar pattern following its oil reserves débacle.

ITALY

Italy has moved towards improving corporate governance in several ways in recent years. It has privatised a number of state-owned enterprises and reformed securities laws and market regulations. In 1998 the Draghi Commission recommended reforms including the discouragement of cross-shareholding for quoted companies, strengthening minority shareholder rights and enabling shareholders to appoint a member of the statutory audit board.

Italy remains a country with an economy driven by smaller companies (like the German Mittelstand) so that reforms have had little impact beyond the quoted sector. In the quoted sector the implosion of Parmalat has revealed the inadequacy of corporate governance in many Italian companies.

SPAIN

Spain has moved some distance towards dismantling the state-owned fabric inherited from the Franco era, but Spanish capitalism remains entangled with cross-shareholdings and 'shareholders of reference' (banks and other corporations). In 1998 the Olivencia Commission issued a report and a code of best practice in corporate governance, which follows the 'soft law' approach of most European codes. The code remains voluntary and is opposed in some respects by investors, especially in respect of independent directors, since most non-executive directors are nominated by 'shareholders of reference' to protect their interests. As a result there is more interest in defining the duties of directors, increasing transparency of board processes, preventing conflicts of interest, fostering shareholder control and strengthening the independence of auditors, rather than appointing independent directors. The Aldama Report of 2003 abandoned the ideal of relating the number of independent directors to the proportion of free float in the share capital.

At the same time the Ley Financera of 2002 has helped to improve the working of financial markets and the independence and rotation of auditors. The Act also provides for an Audit Committee of the board with a majority of external directors. Parliament is developing a Bill to improve transparency in company processes, including an annual report on corporate governance, and to define the duties of directors. Action has also been taken to reform take-over practice and to remove barriers (such as golden shares) which inhibit market efficiency.

SWITZERLAND

Swiss capitalism has differed from other models for many years and overseas investors see Switzerland as 'the fortress of the Alps'. Swiss capitalism has developed for the benefit of Swiss entrepreneurs and has had a very restrictive approach to shareholders. Many Swiss businesses are 'close' companies, with little concern for minorities; often Swiss companies have multiple classes of shareholding, virtually disenfranchising all but core shareholders. In 1992 the Revised Swiss Code of Obligations made basic changes in Swiss law to bring it closer to EU regulations. These changes included:

- improved protection for shareholders and creditors;
- tighter rules on the capital structure of Swiss companies;
- increased transparency of financial reporting; and
- more precision in corporate governance rules (board duties, shareholder meetings, and so on).

In recent years there has been an increase in shareholder activism in Switzerland, prompted in part by scandals such as the failure of Swissair and SBG. The creation of dual nationality companies, such as ABB, has brought new thinking to Swiss managers. The trading of ADR shares in New York (including Novartis and UBS) has also begun to force greater transparency in reporting. Even core Swiss companies, like Nestlé, are beginning to feel the impact of shareholder activism but it may be many years before Swiss managers feel really accountable.

RUSSIA

Russia moved in the mid-1990s from a largely state-owned economy to one which has been looted by the managers of state enterprises and sold out to a limited number of 'oligarchs'. Many of these are now immensely rich and have been able to exploit their companies virtually without constraint, moving funds offshore and investing in other countries. The small number of foreign investors who have sought to partner the oligarchs, for example, BP, have needed to re-think their approach to the Russian market.

In 1999 a Federal Law on the Protection of Rights and Legitimate Interests of Investors in the Securities Market was enacted but has not yet been made effective. In 2000 the Federal Securities Commission started work on a corporate governance code and Russia has stated its intention to adopt International Accounting Standards. The Vasiliev Institute for Corporate Governance was established, with help from State Street Bank and George Soros, in 2000. In 2002 a corporate governance code was introduced and companies are expected from 2003 to report their practices against the code. Pressure from investors, the Russian Institute of Directors and the Vasiliev Institute has led to greater openness in reporting and on websites. The new code will establish bylaws for shareholders' meetings, board and board committee meetings, management board meetings, company secretarial and audit processes, financial control, internal audit, dividend policy and information policy. More than 70 leading Russian companies now have independent directors; the OMZ board now has a majority of independent directors.

Disclosure of ownership remains an issue, although Yukos and LUK, two of Russia's largest companies, have published their shareholding list. Even a few oligarchs are changing their habits, for example, Oleg Deripaska of Russian Aluminium has registered a new acquisition in Russia, not offshore as has been usual for oligarchs. Other issues to be settled in Russian governance include clear rules for mergers, acquisitions, re-organisations, and so on, and for the payment of dividends, board composition, directors' independence and effective governance practices.

The recent attack by the Kremlin on Yukos, claiming unpaid taxes, may be the beginning of a reversal of moves to open Russia to external investment. It has caused severe loss of confidence in corporate governance in Russia in the short term and may lead to an extension of the state sector in selected cases.

CANADA

In 1994 the Dey Committee laid down the foundations for corporate governance in Canada. This work was developed by the Chartered Accountants of Canada report 'Beyond Compliance: Building a Governance Future' published in 2001. The authors claim: 'Our recommendations go beyond compliance and propose guidelines, principles and practices that will help directors build healthy corporate cultures in the board room, where it counts.' There is considerable focus on the working of the company board, whose five core functions are seen to be:

- 'Choosing the CEO and ensuring that the senior management team is sound, focused and capable of successfully managing the company.
- Setting the board parameters within which the management team operates: examples include adopting a strategic planning process and approving a strategic direction; defining a framework to monitor the management of business opportunities and risks; in defined circumstances, approving major corporate decisions, and approving a communications policy that includes a framework for investor relations and a public disclosure policy, which may involve a process for monitoring the relationship between the corporation and investment dealers.
- Coaching the CEO and the management team; the metaphor of a coach is chosen deliberately to underscore that the directors are not players – they should provide direction and advice but they don't do management's job.

- Monitoring and assessing the performance of the CEO, setting the CEO's compensation and approving the compensation of senior management, and taking remedial action where warranted, including replacing the CEO if necessary.
- Providing assurance to shareholders and stakeholders about the integrity of the corporation's reported financial performance.'

The report also focuses on four conditions needed to produce a culture of independence from management:

- 'Strong board members who are independent of management, provided with appropriate orientation, and who bring an appropriately diverse set of experiences, competencies, skills and judgement to the board. We refer to such directors in this report as outside directors.
- Strong leadership within the board from an outside director. We describe the functions that such a director must have as the functions of an 'independent board leader'.
- A CEO who understands the role of the board and is openly supportive of building a healthy governance culture.
- Regular meetings of outside directors without management to build relationships of confidence and cohesion among themselves.'

The concept of an 'independent board leader' equates to that of a 'senior non-executive director' in the UK.

AUSTRALIA

Australia's system of corporate governance is similar to that of the UK and USA in general. Australia has two codes; one based on the Bosch Report of 1995 and sponsored by the Australian Institute of Company Directors, and the other developed in 1999 by the Investment and Financial Services Association. These are aimed at individual organisations as examples of best practice.

Boards in Australia usually have a majority of external directors, but there is no history of independence among them, as these directors have tended to come from a limited pool of inter-linked people. Ownership in Australia is also skewed towards the large financial institutions which again hampers independence. 'Clubbiness' remains at the core of Australian capitalism, despite the dissemination of codes, and Australia has so far failed to emerge as a force in global capitalism. The latest setback, after Broken Hill, AMP, National Australia Bank, and so on, is the incorporation of News Corporation in the USA in place of Adelaide.

In 2002 the Howath Corporate Governance Report was issued, reviewing progress to date. National Australia Bank was equal first, yet is an economic disaster! News Corporation was 122nd, Rio Tinto 120th, so that the message of corporate governance is slow to impact on many major groups, quite apart from a long tail of smaller local companies.

NEW ZEALAND

New Zealand's capitalism has suffered from the 'old boy' syndrome which has affected Australia. New Zealand has also a heavily export-orientated economy which has placed it at the mercy of global economic forces. Like Australia, New Zealand is seeking to 'catch up' with the development of corporate governance in larger economies. In August 2000 the Commonwealth Association for Corporate Governance issued 'Guidelines: Best Practice Statements for Boards and Directors in New Zealand'. In 2003 the New Zealand Stock Exchange released its final recommendations for corporate governance, including a minimum one-third independent directors, separate chairman and CEO, certified qualification of all directors, an audit committee with a majority of independent directors (at least one with an accounting qualification), auditors to rotate lead partner every five years. These rules will become mandatory when approved.

SOUTH AFRICA

The King Report (1994) was the pioneer of corporate governance in Africa and fed into the Commonwealth Association for Corporate Governance Guidelines (1999). The King Code is largely based on the UK Cadbury Code and successors, adapted to meet local conditions. The Institute of Directors in South Africa sponsored the King Report and has established a Commission to monitor progress and update its code. Having been a pariah for many years, South Africa is keen to attract foreign investment, thus the King Code has strong government support. One short-term problem in South Africa is the positive discrimination in favour of black directors, which has obliged many of them to 'learn on the job'. In time this burden is expected to rectify itself and to create a wider pool of talent.

CHINA

China is involved in a wrenching change from state enterprise to capitalism. In principle there is a major shift of resources from the state sector to companies with shareholding. In practice banks continue to support moribund state enterprises and jobs have not shifted to private companies. Many of the joint ventures which have attracted large overseas investment in recent years have state companies as a partner, usually a majority partner, and China lacks institutional investors and analysts to provide and use financial information.

There are four challenges to China as it develops modern capitalism and corporate governance practices to regulate it:

- Reducing the regulatory role of the state and the predominance of state ownership.
- Avoiding 'crony capitalism' or the Russian model in order to retain outside investors.
- Building an institutional investor base to sponsor best practice.
- Strengthening the role of banks in corporate governance.

China has been favoured by the enthusiasm of outside investors for its market potential. Many such investors have been disappointed by their experience in China, often because of lack of market research and due diligence in making acquisitions, so that China will need to improve its governance to maintain the flow of funding needed to sustain its necessarily rapid rate of growth. Recent Chinese interventions in the affairs of Hong Kong raise questions about the balance of political and economic considerations in the minds of China's rulers. It is to be hoped that Chinese pragmatism will ultimately prevail.

Governance – rules based or led by principles?

We have seen how concern about corporate governance has been driven in most markets by investors, and their market place – the stock exchange. In many markets, especially the USA and UK, the spur to action was a series of scandals or abuses (corporate raiders) which destroyed shareholder value. The initial focus of reform was financial, since full and frank financial reporting lies at the heart of trading shares. Lack of openness and accountability has made investment in many developing markets hazardous for outsiders, which has delayed their expansion and integration into the global economy. As we have seen there is now a widening recognition of the need for improved corporate governance in most countries; the sincerity of that recognition may be doubted in some cases, for example, Zimbabwe, but few countries deny the need for the appearance of good governance in order to meet the requirements of the World Bank, IMF and other lenders.

Most countries have developed capitalism with the support of law, which may or may not be enforceable in practice. Company law is the backbone of corporate structures and processes, with other branches of law supporting external relationships, for example, mercantile law with customers. When the Cadbury Commission was working on its Inquiry there was an initial expectation that its findings would be incorporated into company law. Sir Adrian Cadbury felt that informality would be more powerful than legal rules, where it is tempting for those affected to obey the 'letter of the law' and ignore the deeper purpose behind it. As a result the Cadbury Code is not legally binding but the obligation to report against it should reveal which companies are trying to meet its spirit and which are manoeuvring round it. All subsequent codes have the same status and many overseas codes are also voluntary.

Codes with legal enforceability are rules. The USA tends to favour a rules-based approach to corporate governance, since its capital markets are strictly regulated by the SEC. American regulators are quick to take legal action against companies or their officers who are seen to be in breach of regulations, hence the activities of New York Attorney, Eliot Spitzer, in indicting Merrill Lynch and Citigroup for conflict of interest. In 2002 the SEC brought 598 actions against companies and individuals, of which 163 were for financial fraud. The total number of actions increased by 24 per cent over the level in 2001. It may be seen that actions vary from criminal to civil in nature; what is not clear is the extent to which actions were settled out of court or were only threatened.

Principles

At the other extreme lies the principles approach to governance. In Chapter 1 we saw how the Nolan Committee on 'Standards in Public Life' had established a set of seven principles as a touchstone for its inquiry into all aspects of public life. The advantages of principles over rules may be considered to be as follows:

- Principles are easy to understand but are not rigidly defined as are rules.
- Principles relate to individual behaviour in order to shape group behaviour, whereas rules are undifferentiated.
- Principles should have universal acceptance whereas rules may be specific to a given group at a certain point in time.

Principles usually reflect universal values, which are easy to recognise. How those values are interpreted may vary between cultures and individuals. Honesty may be interpreted differently by Mafia members and clergymen. Nor are principles easy to measure; there is no British Standard for integrity. Principles are really touchstones – you can usually recognise them when you meet them, even though it would be difficult to define them in a way which everybody would accept. Rules need to be defined in order to be enforced. Such definition may often involve measurement (as in speed limits) and measurement aids enforcement. Arbitrary rules – 'thou shall not kill' – are open to argument about definition. How is a soldier to react to such a rule? What is the difference between 'kill' and 'help to die'? And so on.

Principles relate to human behaviour and reflect the norms expected of each of us by the rest of society. Where the majority respects a principle it will become the norm and others will be expected to abide by it individually. Where a principle loses general acceptance, for example, the acceptability of slavery, it will be changed by general consent. The strength of principles lies in their general acceptance and their ability to create trust between individuals and within society. Rules are rarely embedded in the human psyche nor do they have the universality associated with principles. Rules are made to regulate the conduct of a specific group at a certain point in time. Often rules are preventative rather than enabling, couched in negative rather than positive terms, and rules tend to change with circumstances. Principles are usually more enduring since they are passed down the generations and become 'hard wired' in our psyche.

Corporate governance within the organisation

In many organisations corporate governance is still seen as 'something done by the company secretary'. Most people are aware of Enron and other scandals well exposed in the media but see them as manifestations of individual and corporate greed in the USA which do not touch them personally. Few employees read the corporate governance section in the annual report of their company nor do most companies make it compelling reading.

How can employees in all parts of the company be brought into its governance? Many companies operate on the basis of a top-down culture which shapes the daily lives of employees in all parts of the organisation. Wal-Mart is a typical example, following the pattern set by Sam Walton and replicated in every new store. As such companies grow the ability to regiment behaviours is reduced; national differences need to be accommodated and individuality recognised in order to attract talent. Wal-Mart has struggled in Germany largely for cultural reasons.

Most companies now recognise the need to appeal to employees, and potential employees, as well as to customers. Where personal freedom is increasing and people have choices in their lives, companies need to engage them and win their support. In many key roles talented employees recruit their employer rather than the reverse. In such a situation the need to integrate corporate governance within the company becomes critical. At the extreme, 'star' employees can hold the company to ransom, for example, in many investment banks.

Inside an organisation, governance is traditionally delivered through the structure and processes which control the flow of instructions and information needed for it to function. The classical model is that of the military, adapted for civilian use, which allocates discretion in proportion to rank in the hierarchy. This 'command and control' model fits ill with the need for flexibility and initiative at all levels in fast-moving modern business.

Strategic planning

One approach to taking corporate governance into an organisation is to harness the strategic planning system. We saw in Chapter 1 how governance is focused on 'purpose'; strategy also flows from 'mission' which is synonymous. If we compare the 'eight dimensions of corporate governance' (Chapter 1) with the equivalent dimensions of the strategy process we have the following picture:

Governance	*Strategy*
Identity	Vision and values
Purpose	Mission
Leadership	Strategic direction
Distribution of power	Resource allocation
Inclusiveness, communication	Reporting and review
Accountability	Targets
Maximising effectiveness	Key action programme
Ensuring sustainability	Innovation, self-renewal

An organisation's 'vision' is the state to which it aspires at some long-term future time, for example, 'The world's favourite retailer' might inspire Morrisons. 'Values' are the personal and group attributes through which the 'vision' may be realised. BAE SYSTEMS cites 'performance – No. 1 priority', 'people', 'innovation and technology', 'customers' and 'partnering' as its values. An organisation's mission describes the means by which it intends to realise its vision. The 'mission statement' of Barclays plc seeks 'to be an innovative, customer-focused Group that delivers superb products and services, ensures excellent careers for our people and contributes positively to the communities in which we live and work'. Reckitt Benckiser plc takes a different approach:

> Our passion is to improve people's lives when they use our household cleaning or health and personal care products. Our power comes from our people, our brands and our focused strategy. It enables us to drive growth and profits harder. Our ultimate purpose is to create shareholder value.

'Strategic direction' points to how the mission will be fulfilled. This is the basic impulsion which guides and combines the various strategies needed to fulfil the mission. Leadership is crucial to the creation and implementation of strategies, not in isolation but with the full involvement of all concerned (that is, all stakeholders). 'Resource allocation' is the process of supporting strategies with finance and human resources in order to implement them successfully. This requires a distribution of resources (in effect, power) in order to maximise effectiveness. 'Reporting and review' covers the feedback of information on progress to date, and the process of adjusting strategies to meet problems or opportunities as they emerge. This requires inclusiveness and effective communication to maximise results. 'Targets' are important in strategy since they enable progress or setbacks to be measured. Targets can be motivating if they have the consent of those who are accountable. A 'key action' programme is an important tool of strategy, since it will define key tasks and the deadlines and accountabilities for delivering them. These key tasks are usually the means of achieving specific targets. Effective organisations place great emphasis on key action programmes.

'Innovation' and 'self-renewal' are the key strategies for ensuring the sustainability of organisations. Innovation applies to products and processes, both to bring novelty and to reduce waste. Self-renewal is the process of discarding old ideas and redundant skills in order to remain intensely competitive, much as the human body is continually discarding dead cells and growing new ones. Innovation and self-renewal are the hallmarks of sustainable organisations. At General Electric the approach is rather Darwinian (survival of the fittest) but it has avoided the sclerosis which has weakened many of its competitors over recent years.

Marketing

The marketing function has increasing importance in most businesses; in the case of those setting fast-moving consumer goods, marketing is usually at the core of the company and branding is the touchstone of success. Marketing focuses primarily on customers or potential customers, and seeks to influence their buying through advertising and targetted promotions. In the context of corporate governance, marketing is supportive of a stakeholder approach to customers but may be less supportive of other stakeholders. Marketing is important for developing and delivering strategy, since the market information used to build strategic plans usually comes through marketing which is usually the key driver of the process of generating revenue. In my experience, marketing people are often impatient of the discipline needed to formulate and deliver strategy, preferring to focus on the excitement of planning advertising campaigns and promotions rather than gearing them to corporate objectives. I wrote at length on this issue in *The Strategic Role of Marketing* (McGraw Hill, 1995) and much remains to be done to make marketers more strategic in their thinking.

The attitude of marketers to corporate governance is ambivalent. Many see it as a remote compliance function which may inhibit their freedom of action. Other marketers recognise the importance of corporate reputation to branding and the danger of damage through poor governance, for example the hesitation of Perrier to respond to a failure of quality. Persuading marketers of the need to work to improve corporate governance is crucially important, since they are often opinion formers within the company and their messages through the media need to reinforce the work done elsewhere in the organisation to effect good governance.

Human resources

Corporate governance is effected by people so that the role of the HR function in encouraging best practice is crucial for success. Many HR departments retain a legacy of the earlier focus on 'industrial relations', in which negotiations with trades unions was their key role. In most organisations today HR departments are a resource to support operations executives in managing and developing their staff. A key feature of this role is to identify and promote best practice, often from totally unrelated businesses, which stimulates better performance and self-improvement. We have seen how organisations can be driven by clear mission and value statements in drafting which HR has an important contribution to make. More significant on a day-to-day basis is the development of a 'code of conduct', based on the values (or business principles) which should guide the behaviour of all employees and agents of the company. An example of this may be seen in Chapter 5 (Diageo plc). The HR function also has a key role in shaping behaviours to match company values, both through training and through regular mentoring programmes and appraisals.

Purchasing

For many years purchasing departments have treated suppliers and contractors as servants of their company rather than as partners. Buying was considered to be an adversarial relationship, with multiple suppliers to create competition, working through instructions rather than discussion, and seeking to minimise commitment and cost. In recent times an increasing number of organisations are developing partnership relationships with suppliers, both to reduce the cost of multiple sourcing and to benefit from shared design and cost reduction programmes. Companies now see suppliers as an extension of their own organisation and seek to optimise communication and IT links with them in order to improve efficiency. Many companies also seek to bring suppliers into their governance orbit as full stakeholders; this recognises the reality that modern relationships depend on openness and accountability. Franker relationships with suppliers requires a will to work with them as equal partners, not as subordinates. It also obliges both partners to share common values and to work together to build shared prosperity. Good corporate governance requires a concerted effort to involve suppliers in the company's processes, led by the purchasing team but with support from the board and a right of appeal to the board if a supplier believes he or she is not receiving fair treatment.

Finance

The finance function is at the heart of corporate governance since it ensures the control of assets and liabilities and provides the figures on which all stakeholders rely. At one time only shareholders could seek legal redress for inaccuracy in published figures; companies now owe a duty of care to anyone who uses their accounts. As the sole official 'scorekeepers', accountancy staff are exposed to pressure from executives who wish to meet targets and qualify for bonuses and from hackers and other fraudsters who wish to steal company assets. Professionalism has been the shield which protected accountants from manipulation, but all professionals today, accountants, lawyers, actuaries and others, are exposed to pressure to satisfy the needs of quarterly reporting and annual targets from chief executives and other executive directors whose power is not properly restrained. This has been seen in companies like Enron, where the CFO was actively involved in manipulation, and Equitable Life where results were actuarially unsustainable.

Particular care is needed, therefore, to put the finance function at the heart of corporate governance. The role of the audit committee, controlled by non-executive directors, has been strengthened in recent times but the focus needs to shift to prevention of misfeasance rather than detection. Misfeasance often occurs where managers use their authority in their own interest rather than in that of the company. A weak company culture encourages misfeasance and manipulation; where companies have strong values and consistent behaviours to match them there is growing evidence, for example, that provided by the Good Company, to show that organisations with strong value systems minimise internal disruptions and increase profitability (see Chapter 7). The Good Company helps companies to establish demanding standards and to carry out bottom-up checks on performance against these standards.

One development which should strengthen the financial function is the development of International Financial Reporting Standards which should bring greater clarity to financial reporting and facilitate international comparisons and cross-boundary audits. Use of the new standards should also lead to fuller disclosure to meet the demands of analysts.

Public relations

Many companies have attempted to treat corporate governance and its extension, corporate social responsibility, as exercises in public relations. Enron had an exemplary corporate governance process but was shown to be 'living a lie'. Too many companies still go through the processes of reporting against the Combined Code without testing their results at all levels of their organisation. Failure to take the Code as a thorough health check means that company directors are never sure how sound are the internal workings of their company nor whether some canker is attacking the roots of their business (as happened with Barings Bank). The requirements of the Turnbull Code and growing concern about corporate reputation, for example, the demise of Arthur Andersen as a result of a series of defective audits, are encouraging boards to commission outside 'health checks' to give them reassurance to back their governance reporting. An example health check approach is that of Strategic Partnership Limited (Appendix D).

Rather than use public relations to 'whitewash' their corporate governance, boards should concentrate on ensuring that their governance is sound at all levels in the company. They should also involve their stakeholders in company events. Annual general meetings are seen as a problem by most company directors but they offer the opportunity of creating an 'open day' atmosphere and of allowing stakeholders to share the event. Who ever invited suppliers to attend their AGM and share lunch with the board and shareholders?

Companies have been attempting to take their corporate governance into the public arena through corporate social responsibility (CSR) activities. This can be an effective way to deliver corporate governance benefits to communities (see Chapter 7, Business in the Community). CSR can be very effective when it is linked to corporate governance objectives, that is, it is for the long-term benefit of the company not just for charity and short-term publicity. Some companies, for example, Shell, have overplayed CSR and neglected the direction of their business. Another dangerous area for companies is sponsorship. Too often this is a way to indulge the interest of directors in the arts, golf or activities which do not relate to the purpose of the company. Part of corporate governance is to bring greater rigour to sponsorship, spending to build the company's future not to indulge the fleeting wishes of its current leaders.

Company secretary/compliance

We have seen some examples of the areas of the company which need to be involved in the routine of corporate governance. Areas which have not been singled out for examination above must also be built into the network. Operational areas, such as manufacturing or trading, are the motors of any company and their need to develop and sustain behaviours in line with the purpose and values of the company is equally compelling. Many businesses are being damaged currently by their failure to train and motivate call centre staff to be ambassadors of the company. No part of any company is too unimportant to be integrated into the corporate governance network.

The centre of this network in a typical company will be the company secretary or a compliance function linked to the board, often through the company secretary. An example of such a function at work is shown in the case study about Diageo, and this is echoed in other case studies such as The Carphone Warehouse. Compliance is often linked to risk management in order to integrate reporting. For compliance to be effective the company secretary or compliance officer must be supported from the top and at all levels. The processes to deliver compliance must be rigorous, capable of measurement and reach all parts of the organisation. Reporting standards must be consistent in all circumstances, though nominal variations may be explained. Without consistent scoring, comparisons across the company become impossible – even with consistent scoring there will be anomalies which need to be ironed out or explained. Consistent scoring is essential in order to judge the performance of teams and individuals – people will accept rigour provided that the process demonstrates fairness.

The future progress of corporate governance depends crucially on the ability to engage the commitment of people in all parts of the organisation, and among its stakeholders, to making it a practical reality. At present most corporate governance is symbolic and systemic – it has engaged some minds but very few hearts. Individuals need to be involved and be free to express their views, and, if necessary, 'blow the whistle' so that the integrity of governance can be protected.

3 Leadership and Corporate Governance

Few concepts have caused more confusion than that of leadership. When societies were isolated and focused on survival it was natural for the best hunter to assume leadership of the group and for the others to be ordered in a hierarchy to provide support. Later leaders were expected to demonstrate wisdom, and seniority by age became a key criterion of leadership (supported by a caste of priests – the precursors of today's management consultants!). In ancient Egypt the pharoahs were expected to ensure the annual flooding of the Nile Valley; Roman emperors were expected to make conquests and provide booty – throughout history there has been some form of pact between leaders and their followers to reflect their mutual dependence. Even 'absolute' monarchs like Darius and Louis XIV had to underpin their position by manipulation and largesse.

The concept of leadership has been confused with that of heroism, creating the Nelson syndrome. Frederick the Great fought in most of his battles, like a medieval monarch, which won the affection of his soldiers. Scott of the Antarctic was heroic in an adversity which his own poor planning had created. Heroic leadership is a model of leadership which has tended to overshadow other ways of being a leader.

It may be useful to attempt to segment leadership into different models. There are at least five distinct manifestations of leadership in a spectrum from individual to collective motivation:

- Heroic leadership (for example, Nelson)
- Crisis leadership (for example, company doctor)
- Collegiate leadership (for example, partners, university, and so on)
- Servant leadership – empowering others
- Transformational leadership – effecting major change.

Heroic leadership

As we have seen this is the 'Hollywood model' of leadership, succeeding against the odds in a personal mission. Heroic leaders have charisma and can engage others to follow their mission. The outcome is usually impactful and, at the extreme limit, can be tragic, for example Adolf Hitler. Heroic leaders have followers, rarely partners. Their agenda is personal and often focused on self-aggrandisement, for example, Jean-Marie Messier of Vivendi. Heroic leaders do not like to contemplate issues of succession – who within Disney can realistically follow Michael Eisner? Strong leaders often fail to establish the governance structure needed to ensure their legacy, as the decline of Coca-Cola begins to show.

Heroic leadership is not only found in those with a flamboyant style but is equally manifest in organisations which have been captured by quietly resolute egocentrics. Lord Weinstock made GEC his personal fiefdom and only made significant changes as a reaction to the threat of a take-over bid. John Ritblat helped to create British Land and has controlled it totally ever since.

The essence of heroic leadership is the lack of any alternative. It may succeed in the short term, but it depends on the judgement of one person so that there is no process for 'reality checking' its goals or developing new leaders. Heroic leadership brooks no challenge, yet challenge is the essential counter balance of true leadership. Heroic leadership rarely has effective succession

Crisis leadership

Crisis leadership has many of the characteristics of heroic leadership – the concentration of power, the suspension of alternative sources of leadership and the focus on loyalty. Some heroic leaders begin as crisis leaders, for example, Lee Iacocca at Chrysler, but the essence of crisis leadership is that it is temporary. The typical crisis leader is the 'company doctor' installed by receivers to rescue failing businesses. Such operators need to diagnose problems quickly, reduce expenditure without delay and 'weed out' under-performing staff. This is process leadership at its most rapid, focused on rescue and discounting the future.

The qualities needed for crisis leadership equate with those of war leaders. A steely sense of purpose is paramount, with minimal consideration of the consequences of action and cursory evaluation of alternative tactics. Since few crisis leaders are also business developers, they normally move on to a fresh challenge after their intervention. Many, however, fail to install a successor capable of growing the company after its rescue, hence the decline of the Thomas Cook Group after the departure of Tom Fisher in 1980.

Collegiate leadership

It is rare to have all of the qualities of leadership in one person (the sense of purpose, the will to succeed, the ability to build a coalition and sustain it and the foresight to build for the future). The skills of envisioning, advocacy and negotiation need to be married to unswerving determination, resilience and manoeuvrability. Organisations which concentrate leadership, such as the armed services, place people in leadership positions who may not be effective leaders. The senseless slaughter in the trenches during the First World War is evidence of this failure. For some organisations the concentration of leadership is counter productive. Membership groups work by collaboration not hierarchy; such groups include co-operatives and mutual societies, as well as most charities. Many professional firms are still structured as partnerships, so that the senior partner is only *primus inter pares*. Universities are run on collegiate lines which require consultation and consensus before major decisions are made. All of these are different models of collegiate leadership which shares power among those who have responsibility for part of the organisation in order to negotiate a consensus for action.

Collegiate leadership has many critics; some fear that it produces suboptimal decisions, even confusing ones – 'a camel is a horse designed by a committee'. The process of collegiate leadership is taxing for the nominal leader – Leo Murray, former Director of Cranfield

Business School, likened the process to 'herding cats'. Collegiate leadership is slow, frustrating and difficult to bring to conclusion – like democracy it is messy but legitimate.

Servant leadership

Servant leadership is an ancient idea which has re-emerged into a modern world. The idea that leaders are answerable to their followers is at the heart of the tribal system and later leaders who failed to meet expectations, such as the pharoah at the time when the Nile failed to flood, lost their authority and usually their life. The gesture of Christ in washing the feet of his disciples was a demonstration of servant leadership. He was showing that leaders and their followers are interdependent; he was also preparing them to take responsibility when he was no longer physically present. A key facet of servant leadership is helping followers to grow in stature and become leaders themselves.

In Hermann Hesse's book *Journey to the East*, a group of travellers set out under the guidance of a servant who disappears, leaving them to find their own way ahead. Events seem to conspire to favour their progress but only when they take control. In the end they complete the journey, having learned a great deal (not least about themselves) and are re-united with their servant.

This concept of servant leadership has been developed in a business context by Robert Greenleaf, who founded The Greenleaf Center for Servant Leadership in 1964. It is interesting to contrast the ten characteristics of a servant leader as selected by Greenleaf's acolyte Larry Spears in *Focus on Leadership* (Wiley, 2002) with those identified by Warren Bennis to typify 'tomorrow's leader':

Greenleaf	*Bennis*
Listening	Bias towards action
Empathy ⎫	
Healing ⎭	Leadership of women
Awareness	Self-awareness and self-esteem
Persuasion	Generate trust
Conceptualisation	Great vision with meaning
Foresight	Purpose and vision
Stewardship	Act big if small – act small if big
Commitment to growth of people ⎫	
Building community ⎭	Make federations of corporations
	Comfortable with technology
	Porous and permeable boundaries

Although there is much common ground, it is intriguing to note the relative passivity of the Greenleaf list, compared with the purposeful tone of that of Warren Bennis. Why is 'trust' mentioned by Bennis and not by Greenleaf?

At a time when the USA has an aggressively 'masculine' President, it is interesting to note the emphasis in both lists on 'feminine' characteristics. To use another model, it is as if servant-leadership invited us to use the right-hand side of the brain (creativity, intuition, conceptualisation) as well as the left-hand side (calculation, analysis) – the traditional source of leadership.

Dr Rubye Howard Braye re-orders the ten Greenleaf characteristics as follows:

Self	*Relationships*	*Tasks/resources*
Awareness	Listening	Stewardship
Foresight	Empathy	
Conceptualisation	Healing	
	Persuasion	
	Commitment to growth of others	
	Building community	

This framework matches Danah Zohar's three levels of intelligence (*Rewiring the Corporate Brain*, Berret-Koehler, 1997):

Spiritual intelligence	Emotional intelligence	Intellectual intelligence

Whereas most leadership has focused primarily on tasks and resources, using relationships to deliver the tasks, few leaders have mastered the area of self. The focus is on doing not on being. The thesis of servant leadership is that being is the foundation for effective doing. Being creates an inner necessity – 'this has to happen. I have to do it.' It may be triggered by an opportunity or by a crisis but the compulsion comes from deep inside the psyche. This drove Bernard Palissy to ruin his life to discover the secret of enamel and Captain Scott to perish in an attempt to reach the South Pole. More far reaching was the crusade against slavery of William Wilberforce and the passive resistance of Mahatma Gandhi to British rule in India.

As we have seen, the modern concept of servant leader seems to originate in Hermann Hesse's *Journey to the East*. At one level this is a version of Barrie's 'Admirable Crichton' yet it demonstrates that being a servant to the core of your nature can enable you to become an effective leader. In the words of St Matthew: 'whoever wants to be great among you must be your servant', as was typified by Christ washing the feet of his disciples.

One model of servant leadership which is well established is stewardship. This is reflected in the role of trustees of charities and philanthropic institutions; in fact, it is the true role of any individual or group of individuals who acts on behalf of a beneficiary. This is the true role of company directors, who are stewards for the shareholders, not de facto owners of the company (although too many behave as if they were!). It is interesting that the Nolan principles of governance in the public sector reflect well the concept of servant leadership, comprising openness, honesty, accountability, integrity, selflessness, objectivity and leadership. The principles which underline the Hampel, Cadbury and Greenbury Codes do not include objectivity and selflessness! Servant leaders of the world will need to unite to close that gap!

Transformational leadership

Transformational leadership is manifest in effecting major change. The re-birth of South Africa as a multi-ethnic nation was due to transformational leadership from Nelson Mandela and F. W. de Klerk, supported by patient work by many thousands inside and outside South Africa. Transformational leadership often requires a figurehead leader to integrate and drive the process; in heroic leadership the focus is on the leader, in transformational leadership the leader is an instrument of change.

At the beginning of the 1990s, IBM was on the edge of insolvency. It had failed to adapt to the change from integrated to distributed computing and focused on hardware rather than software. Worse, it had a culture of technological excellence and failed to listen to its customers. In April 1993 Lou Gerstner, formerly CEO of R J R Nabisco and earlier of American Express, brought as its new chairman and CEO a marketing culture which was totally foreign to 'the IBM way'. Gerstner opened up IBM, by making customer contact a key priority and by meeting customers himself all over the USA. Employees were driven out of their offices onto the road working with laptop computers, and working in customer premises to deal with their problems. Gerstner ended plans to dismantle IBM but shifted the focus from products to solutions, so that systems integration (not always with IBM products) became the driver of the business. To enable the new IBM to succeed, Gerstner broke down national 'baronies' and built an organisation based on 14 customer sectors (retailing, financial services, government, and so on). Compensation was geared to the success of the whole company, rather than to the parochial success of business units. This created an integrated, outward-looking culture, dedicated to solving customer problems.

Gerstner's success was due in part to the climate of crisis which he found on arrival but he was not hailed as a saviour; rather he met scepticism about his lack of information and communications technology (ICT) knowledge. The main reason for his success was that he opened the doors and windows at IBM and built alliances with customers to offer them a totally new deal. By changing customer expectations and obliging IBM's culture to change in order to meet them, he transformed a moribund company into a new revolutionary force.

Another example of transformational leadership is that of Stanley Fink, CEO of the MAN Group. In the 1990s MAN Group was a conglomerate, built round a 250-year-old sugar business which integrated West Indian plantations with processing and trading. Around this business there had grown up an insurance broking business, a share broking activity and a derivatives operation to support trading. At the time MAN Group languished near the bottom of the FTSE 350 and lacked strategic direction. Stanley Fink decided to challenge each of his four divisions through a scenario planning exercise to decide which of four different scenarios for the next 20 years was most appropriate for its business. At the end of the exercise each had chosen a different scenario, demonstrating different appetites for risk and incompatible cultures. This revelation enabled Stanley Fink to transform the group, selling the sugar business (now trading as E and F Man) and both broking businesses. Derivatives was seen as the new core of the group and MAN Group is now the largest derivatives business in Europe and near the top of the FTSE 100.

The airline industry has been radically changed by the slow and patient success of South West Airlines. The company commenced operations in 1971, dedicated to a low cost, no frills, on time and friendly approach to flying. Its first CEO, Herb Kelleher, saw the business as a family affair, comprising dedicated and friendly staff and a growing band of regular passengers. He wanted flying to be a pleasure rather than a challenge, and he wanted to make it available to a whole new set of passengers who had never before afforded to fly. To do so he needed to set new standards of efficiency and to attract recruits who were willing to work for lower wages than those offered by his competitors and to undertake an unlimited range of tasks. Kelleher succeeded in this endeavour because he created a culture in which staff took pleasure in giving service beyond limits (one hostess drove a stranded passenger home through the night and reported for duty the next morning). Humour was a key factor to building customer relations – the staff would play tricks on passengers, such as hiding in luggage lockers and jumping out unexpectedly. South West Airlines is loyal to its staff, having never had a redundancy exercise or wages cut; it is loyal to its customers and encourages frequent flying. As a result South West Airlines is the most consistently profitable US airline and is a model for low-cost airlines worldwide. Herb Kelleher not only transformed the flying experience for millions but transformed the expectation of all airline passengers worldwide.

Another transformational leader is Charles Dunstone, CEO of The Carphone Warehouse. His contribution to shaping the telephone business is detailed in Chapter 5. He not only created an open market place for mobile telephones but has also begun to transform the fixed-line telephone market.

Transformational leadership is strategic in nature. It requires a clear vision of a better solution to a difficult problem, the will to persuade others to make the changes needed to implement it, and the patience to work, often for many years, to make the transformation. Innovation is one of the key tools of transformational leadership; it was the persistent drive for innovation which turned Nokia from an undistinguished engineering company into world leader in the manufacture of mobile telephones.

Leadership and corporate governance

Having examined the nature of leadership and some different ways in which it is exercised, it will be useful to explore the relationship between leadership and corporate governance. A simplistic approach would be to see leadership as a manifestation of 'animal spirits' and corporate governance as a restraint upon their free expression. This view was shared by many industrialists at the time of the Cadbury Report and resurfaces after each wave of scandal dies down. Sarbanes-Oxley is now under attack from business interests in the USA as an 'over-reaction' to the Enron wave of scandals. The tension between regulation and deregulation is an essential element in sustaining a balanced society; corporate governance is self regulation and it requires leadership to make it effective. Leadership and corporate governance are at their best when they are symbiotic.

Unfortunately the link between leadership and corporate governance is not strong. This is partly because corporate governance has become a self-generating process rather than a minimalist, reporting 'by exception', approach to encouraging good behaviour. Because so many corporate governance activists supported by the media operate by public challenge rather than discreet influence, many business leaders find themselves 'on the back foot' in dealing with governance issues. Their response is too often driven by resentment rather than by commitment to better practice. Pressure from a wider range of activists has forced many companies to embrace 'corporate social responsibility' (CSR), a commitment to community and charitable work which often extends beyond the obligations of corporate governance. Movements such as Business in the Community (see Chapter 7) are a useful vehicle for delivering the stakeholder commitments of corporate governance. Some companies, however, see CSR as a vehicle for public relations and issue elaborate annual reports on their social and ecological activities. Leadership of a business requires that its efforts are focused on the purpose of the enterprise, not on the purpose of those who interact with it. Good corporate governance helps to engage stakeholders without losing sight of the company's own vital interests.

Leadership provides the motivation and impetus to make corporate governance effective. Its key role is to create a culture in the organisation which uses effective governance to achieve its purpose. This culture encourages the behaviours needed to embed corporate governance in the organisation. It may be useful to identify the key elements of governance and the appropriate leadership response to each:

Governance	*Leadership response*
Dispersion of power	Empower widely
Accountability	Give and obtain commitment
Openness	Communicate freely
Integrity	Set an example
Honesty	Set and monitor standards rigorously
Objectivity	Establish checks and balances
Selflessness	Use servant leader approach
Fair rewards	Motivate by opportunity rather than just money
Look to long term	Think and act strategically

It will be seen that most of the governance criteria are Nolan principles. More significantly the seventh Nolan principle is leadership which turns the principles into actions, thus completing the process.

Where does the leadership needed to make governance effective come from? In any organisation it is top management which sets the agenda and the rules for implementing it. In a company the board should fulfil this role, first by establishing the values as principles through which the company will be run and subsequently ensuring that their behaviour, and that of others in the company, consistently reflects those values or principles. In establishing the values the board should involve all parts of the company so that the values are shaped and endorsed by employees for future use. This is often done by 'cascading' through the organisation, using workshops involving people who work together and feeding back reactions so that the values can be tuned to build support.

A new approach

More important for accommodating entrepreneurs to corporate governance is the need to move corporate governance from a 'box-ticking' examination to an open process of building trust. Corporate governance is only a means towards the end of enabling different parties to work together with confidence; the real proof of success is a business with sustainable growth. Growth is at the heart of entrepreneurialism, so that entrepreneurs need to be encouraged, sustained and rewarded for success but only on condition that they work openly with other stakeholders and share the burdens and excitement of building the business with them. To do so means sharing power and recognising the contribution of others to success – could Adrian Cadbury have been thinking of entrepreneurs when he pressed for the separation of the roles of chairman and chief executive in his code?

How can leadership be developed throughout the organisation?

We have examined different forms of leadership and their interplay with corporate governance. We have considered family companies and their long-term leadership and the dynamic and often impatient leadership of entrepreneurs. Following our analysis we may perhaps be able to synthesise the essence of leadership in a business context (for the military it may be significantly different) and begin to understand how to replicate it to raise the performance of an organisation in a remarkable and sustainable fashion.

Leadership for the future is likely to differ from past models. More than 40 years ago, Douglas McGregor of MIT wrote about the contrast between 'Theory X' and 'Theory Y' management. 'Theory X' management is based on 'command and control' techniques developed by the military. In modern terms it reflects a 'driving' approach to leadership, rather than the 'building' approach typified by 'Theory Y'. In his book *The Engaging Leader* (Dearborn Trade, 2003), Ed Gubman contrasts 'drivers' with 'builders':

Drivers	*Builders*
Put results first	Put people and processes first
Stress economic values above everything else	Stress organisation's capabilities
Make decisions	Get others involved
'Crack the whip' (focus on accountability and sanctions)	Let solutions emerge
Focus on 'what' and 'when'	Focus on 'who' and 'how'
Take short-term focus	Take a long-term focus
Get 'on your feet' a lot	Stay 'behind the scenes' more
Are more critical than positive	Are more positive than critical

The 'driver' model of leadership has been encouraged by increasing pressure from institutional investors for constantly improving quarterly results. At a time of growing competition and low interest rates, this has led many CEOs into risky take-overs in order to grow results faster than internal growth would permit. It has even led to fraudulent and semi-fraudulent behaviour, such as off-balance sheet borrowing, resulting in a rash of scandals following the false Millennium boom. Driving CEOs such as Jack Welch are now less able to extract premium results from mature businesses and many business leaders are now 'buying out' their companies or key components of them, in order to avoid the short-term treadmill. One of the key incentives used by driving CEOs has been stock options – with poorer results these are less interesting and the possibility that they will have to be expensed by the company when vested will make them less of a 'free gift'.

It may be that, at a time when 25 per cent of US workers are 'free agents' and that loyalty of key workers commands an increasing price, leaders will need to learn how to engage their workforce more personally. There is a growing shortage of talented people in business and the 'star system' is moving from the investment banks into wider areas of the economy. Talent should not be confused with genius; in Ed Gubman's words: 'Genius does what it must, talent does what it can.' Genius in business is concentrated among entrepreneurs, since a genius is not willingly constrained to recognise external considerations. Businesses often borrow genius, they rarely own it. Leaders need to understand the difference between genius and talent and engage them differently. A business with a strong core of talented people can accommodate and benefit from a small number of colleagues with genius – the reverse would be total bedlam!

According to Ed Gubman, talented people want freedom, control of their tasks, accountability and caring relationships. If talented people are selected carefully to fit with the culture of the company and are encouraged to take risks and grow in competence they will become key building blocks in a dynamic organisation. Companies of the future will see a higher turnover of staff as people increasingly work for themselves. Leaders will need to build a core of dedicated talent, and it will be their leadership which retains this 'band of brothers' (and sisters). Around this core will be a constant flow of 'free agents', lending their talent and learning for their time in the company. Managing such 'birds of passage' will be a new dimension of leadership. If they have big egos they will need to be tamed or depart (big egos destroy trust in an organisation); if they have genius they will leave their mark. Others will need to be given challenging opportunities to move the company forward and to build their curriculum vitae at the same time.

Ed Gubman focuses on sports leadership as a model for business. Sports professionals usually have a short working life and need to drive rapidly for peak performance. Business executives have traditionally had longer careers and have been 'slow growing timber'. The burn-out caused by the 'star' system (borrowed from sport) and the growth of 'free agency' may cause the two models to overlap increasingly. Another interesting analogy is found in *The Leader's Voice* by Boyd Clarke and Ron Crossland (Select Books, 2002) which focuses on the need for leaders to communicate. They cite the success of 'horse whisperers', such as Monty Roberts ('the man who listens to horses') as a method of winning co-operation through a shared language rather than by 'breaking'. They see the process of persuasion used by leaders as having three stages: firstly, the need to collect and present facts to engage the intellect of followers, secondly to appeal to their emotion by identifying with their concerns and aligning them with the task to be shared, and thirdly by agreeing on symbols to encapsulate the total relationship. Symbols are crucially important, like a flag to a regiment or a brand to a trusted product.

This model of leadership and others explored above demonstrate that servant leadership is supplanting the hierarchical approach which has dominated in the past. Leaders now have to be coaches and in some situations even followers, for example, when others have knowledge or experience which they lack. Britain has world leadership in Formula 1 racing cars because it has the resilience to learn from losing (there is only one winner in a race) and the tenacity to innovate fast and radically. Manufacturers of ordinary cars feed from the experience of Formula 1 but they take three to five years to produce a new model. In Formula 1 a new model may be needed in a few weeks. To succeed in Formula 1 a team has to think like a come-back loser.

Where, then, is the essence of leadership for the future? From our analysis it would seem that leaders need to be:

- engaging
- creative
- adaptable
- skilled in coaching and learning
- able to ride risk (like a surf board)
- a model of integrity
- focused on the future.

LEADERSHIP AND RISK

Leadership in war is most tested when the followers and their leader put their lives at risk. Risk is a crucial test of leadership in a business context since a decision may risk the future of the company and the jobs (and reputation) of those involved. Risk emerged as a key dimension of corporate governance with the publication of the Turnbull Report in 1999. This has led to the appointment of executives to manage risk in many larger companies, often along the lines of the compliance officers in banks and other regulated bodies.

Risk is an essential element of any trading activity. For companies it builds profits above the level of deposit interest but exposes them to losses if trading assumptions are incorrect. The higher the tolerance of risk in trading the greater the potential for profit or loss. How should leadership address issues of risk?

The first task for a leader is to ensure that his or her organisation understands the forces shaping its market place and how they may offer threats or opportunities for trading. Most risk assessment is based on previous experience and risk management will seek to set limits on the exposure of the organisation to trading risks. Real leaders will, however, wish to look beyond past experience and explore new and alternative patterns of risk. Businesses do not prosper by copying each other but by innovating and changing the boundaries of their present market place. The Bank of Scotland was concerned how to enter the English market which was already over-branched by competitors. Through a scenario planning study led by St Andrews Management Institute they decided to develop telephone banking – a low-cost, low-risk investment which changed their posture in the market place. While most companies see only the risks they have experienced, some are beginning to use scenario planning to descry risks which are over the horizon. A client of St Andrews Management Institute in the Far East was able to pick up faint signals of potential meltdown early in 1997 and foresee the Asian financial crisis.

Leaders will be alert to potential changes in risk patterns and to the opportunities and threats they may bring. The focus of the Turnbull Report was largely on the protection of physical assets and controlling trading risks. In passing it mentions reputational risk; very quickly most business people saw reputational risk as the biggest single issue in risk management. Scandals in major companies since then, such as Enron and Parmalat, have reinforced this perception. Why is reputational risk so important to companies?

Most successful companies have a share value significantly higher than the net asset value of their balance sheet. This represents the market value of discounted future returns and reflects intangible assets, for example, brands, patents, and so on, rather than physical assets. Reputation underpins such valuations but is at the mercy of the whim of customers. Marks & Spencer thought it had an unassailable position in the market place but lost the trust of its customers. Arthur Andersen was implicated in the collapse of Enron after earlier failures as auditor. It disappeared within weeks as its operating units sold themselves to rivals. Leaders need to be constantly alert to issues which may affect their corporate reputation. This is a strategic task with daily concerns and requiring constant vigilance. It is good reputation which provides the climate in which leadership can thrive.

4 *Implementing Corporate Governance*

Looking at the history of corporate governance, it is striking that the initiative for progress has almost invariably come from external sources, not from organisations themselves. The process begun by the Cadbury Report, and reinforced stage by stage to the current controversy surounding the Higgs Report, has rarely been embraced by companies and has failed to impact at all on many smaller firms. This is both a failure of leadership in most companies and a reflection on the conflicts of interest (between the short and long term, between personal advantage and the interests of the company, and so on) which have never been confronted effectively. These failures have encouraged the external perception that companies are run by a small clique of greedy individuals who are usurping ownership of their assets.

Where does responsibility for corporate governance lie? Although many critics, such as Ralph Ward (*Saving the Corporate Board*, Wiley, 2003), see boards as having declined in effectiveness, they remain legally responsible for directing companies and most rise to the challenge of implementing corporate governance effectively. Leadership for corporate governance must come from the board if it is to fulfil its statutory obligations. Where the board fails to provide leadership, it will be imposed from other sources, usually externally. These may be regulators, such as the FSA in the case of pensions mis-selling, or institutional shareholders in the case of Shell and Sainsbury's. Increasingly the Press challenges leadership vacuums, for example, British Land, though action can only be taken by stakeholders.

A basic model for implementing corporate governance

How can the board drive the process of creating effective governance? One approach to this challenge is shown in Chapter 5, where the new board of Diageo saw effective corporate governance both as a catalyst for merging its constituent companies, Guinness and Grand Metropolitan, and as a means of meeting public disquiet about its market power and the role of alcohol in society. From this case study, and from general principles, it is possible to develop a basic model for implementing corporate governance, whose key elements are:

1 Leadership
2 Culture
3 Structure
4 Processes
5 Brand.

It may be useful to explore these key elements in more detail.

LEADERSHIP

We have examined the roles of leadership in corporate governance in Chapter 3. Its importance cannot be exaggerated but it can only be sustainably effective if it is replicated in all parts of an organisation. Leadership from one person is identified with that individual and is difficult to sustain. Leadership needs to be replicated throughout an organisation to be effective and needs to be identified with the organisation, not one individual. The power of belief is derived from allegiance beyond Jesus, Mohammed, and identified leaders, to a wider and unseen concept. The 'leader' is servant to a cause greater than himself.

Leadership in corporate governance needs to come from the board of directors of a company to have both legitimacy and impact. In an article in *Strategic Change* (June/July, 2002) entitled 'Leadership Boards of Directors', Paul Joyce, Graham Beaver, Adrian Woods and I set out the case for a more challenging approach by company boards to directing their companies strategically. This involves the board actively in the development of strategy, with input from management, rather than leaving strategy formulation to management alone. A study by Judge and Zeithamel in 1992 of 42 organisations shows that companies with the greatest board involvement in strategy formulation and evaluation tended to have high performance. To do this effectively it is necessary to define the roles of both executive and non-executive directors and improve their interaction. It is also necessary to develop better processes for working with shareholders and other external stakeholders, in which non-executive directors take the lead, whereas operational management is led by executive directors with appropriate feedback and controls. The article recommends that company law should make boards responsible for strategic leadership from formulation through ensuring implementation to the evaluation of results. It also recommends a Scrutiny Committee of the board to evaluate performance and the effectiveness of strategic plans in driving it.

I believe, like Ralph Ward, that the first step in board leadership is the appointment of an effective chairperson. It is the chairperson's task to build, develop and manage the board. This requires them to lead the processes of selection, personal development and tasking of each director, and to trigger retirements as appropriate, with the consent of the board. The chairperson should take the initiative in appointing the CEO (and dismissing them if necessary). Too many chairpeople are overshadowed by dominating CEOs, and combining the posts in US and many other companies has led to the confusion of two distinct roles. The chairperson should lead the board and the CEO should lead management. The board is the nexus of internal processes and external relationships (shareholders, stakeholders, and so on) and provides direction to the company in its widest context. To lead this crucial body effectively, the chairperson must have a strong character, board experience and wisdom. A well-chosen CEO will bring enthusiasm and energy to his or her task of working with fellow directors to shape strategy and to lead the teamwork needed to implement it successfully.

Leadership for corporate governance comes from the board. As leader of the board the chairperson has a key role in ensuring that this leadership is forthcoming and sustained. Since most chairpeople today work part-time, they need to focus on setting the scene and monitoring progress rather than driving the implementation of governance processes personally. Given the primacy of the chairpeople's position in the company it is important that they take every opportunity on both public and private occasions to demonstrate their commitment to effective corporate governance. Leadership by example is more powerful than a thousand speeches. An example of how a chairperson should build an effective board may be found in Chapter 5 (Scottish and Southern Energy plc).

Running the board in an open and effective manner is one of the best examples to set for all parts of the company. Meetings should be scheduled well in advance and attendance should be expected from all directors unless there is an unavoidable clash of priorities. If directors are not punctilious in attending meetings, employees will assume that their attendance is not a commitment. Absenteeism figures show that private companies lose over £1 billion per year through unauthorised absence from work. Failure to set a good example from the top can be very expensive.

Leadership should also be shown by the board in its interpersonal relationships. Too many directors believe that aggressive behaviour towards colleagues makes them appear strong. In fact, such behaviour diverts attention from the issues facing the board and makes it harder to build a consensus on how to deal with them. The chairperson has a key role in setting the tone for meetings involving directors – emphasising the need to focus on issues and put personal feelings aside in doing so. This does not mean that board meetings should not be challenging but the challenge should be civilised and focused on issues, not personalities.

The board's leadership will need to be manifest in establishing and maintaining the system needed to effect corporate governance. This system will need to encompass structure, processes, the culture to animate them and to build long-term brand value. These elements are explored further below.

CULTURE

Culture is the shared view of life which binds groups of people together. Tribes are defined by a shared culture and their culture is composed of values and beliefs which they hold in common. In the daily routine, culture is taken for granted and is virtually invisible; culture emerges strongly in times of war or of competition. The haka of the New Zealand rugby players is calculated to terrify their opponents!

In a company, culture is as important in defining its singularity as the pride and uniform of an army regiment. The armed services use culture to engender total loyalty to the unit for whose members each colleague must be willing to die. Such unquestioning loyalty is no longer required of company employees, though it had its place in the East India Company and in building global multi-nationals such as Shell and Unilever. *Esprit de corps* is more difficult to build and sustain in an age where most employees see themselves as 'free agents' and hire their services to a company as a stage in developing a winning résumé. Nevertheless such employees are very choosy in deciding for which company to work and their choice is significantly affected by the culture and reputation of the company concerned. Each year *Fortune* surveys the companies most favoured by their employees ('Great Companies to Work For', 2 February 2004).

How does a company define its culture? The roots of a company's culture grow logically out of its vision, mission and values. 'This is what we want to be, how we intend to achieve it and the values we share in doing it'. The vision states what the company ultimately wants to be – 'we intend to be world market leader in travel finance'. Its mission might be to develop a world market share of X per cent market share by 2050, and to achieve Y per cent market share in wholesale foreign currency exchange and Z per cent retail market share by 2030. Since both vision and mission are projected long term, any company which sought to make unsustainable quick gains or failed to build confidence among its customers through 'sharp practice' would be doomed to fail before long. It is the values of a company which help to build confidence among customers and other stakeholders and it is the behaviours of employees which underpin that confidence. A company's culture is largely defined by the interplay between its values and the behaviour of its employees. Where this becomes embedded in the company's operations it can build enormous goodwill, as for South West Airlines.

If vision, mission and values are the roots of culture, what is its flowering? Reputation is the flowering of the interaction of vision, mission and values. Reputation is slow to grow but is able to continue flowering if well nurtured by its roots. Like any plant, reputation is subject to the threat of disease or external harm. Companies need to nurture their reputation constantly through maintaining behaviours which reflect their values and focusing on their vision and mission. This develops a company's culture, and reputation is the flowering of that culture.

STRUCTURE

Structure is the skeleton, or framework, which supports a company's operations. Its basic manifestation is the organisation chart which itemises the constituents of the company and their relationship to each other. Traditionally this has been presented as a hierarchy with the board at the top and services at the bottom. Cultural sensitivities have created organisation charts with customers at the top, supported by the services of the company. However it is presented, a company needs a logical and understandable structure to support its operations.

Structure is important in governance since it defines the shape and boundaries of an organisation and the inter-relationship between its elements. Structure enables individuals to locate themselves in the company and identify their own inter-relationships. With the support of job descriptions, structure enables employees to identify the people to whom they owe services and from whom they may expect support.

In a company there will be a formal structure (departments, committees, and so on) and informal structures (project teams, ad hoc committees, support groups, and so on). Few companies are adept at mapping the informal relationships which are often more influential than those imposed by the organisation chart. In terms of corporate governance these relationships should not be neglected as there will be accountabilities to be identified and monitored. One of the challenges of corporate governance is to identify and monitor informal relationships and patterns of influence which may affect a company's operations. There is a parallel with the phenomenon of 'shadow directors' whose activities are now covered by the 1985 Companies Act. People who exercise influence without authority need to be caught in the net of governance and restrained.

Structure needs to be clear, open and unambiguous. Directors need to be on constant guard against 'old Spanish customs' or other unauthorised practices which distort accountability. Another phenomenon which needs attention is the Internet. As dictatorial governments worldwide know, the Internet is impossible to control effectively and opens enormous new horizons for all organisations. Corporate governance is not, hopefully, a process supporting dictatorship, but the Internet presents new and unexplored challenges to governance. An obvious example is the danger of staff using the Internet for personal purposes, often pornography, and neglecting their duty. Computer systems can be disrupted by viruses downloaded from the Internet and can also be flooded with junk mail. Even worse are lapses of control which allow company systems to be hacked or files to be stolen. Effective computer systems are a key part of company structure and their protection involves both exacting operating protocols and a culture of responsibility among users.

Structure, for some people, is often neglected in managing companies. Like the infrastructure of a railway it is big and unexciting. Like a railway it has to be reliable to allow traffic to use it with confidence. In a company that traffic is mainly processes.

PROCESSES

Processes drive a company and allow it to function. They can also be seen as the lifeblood which sustains it. Most processes work in 'steady state' so that they are fixed in purpose and way of operating, until modified or updated. Processes can, however, be corrupted and degraded and constant vigilance is needed to avoid this danger. Processes are the main means of taking action and achieving results for a company and deserve more respect and attention then they usually enjoy.

In essence, processes are a series of steps which begin with collecting data relevant to a purpose, process it to extract new meaning and end with a conclusion relevant to that purpose. Rather as in geometry, a process generates a useful answer – *quod erat demonstrandum* (what was required to be demonstrated). The form, extent and content of a process will vary considerably but all have a clear beginning and sufficient steps to produce a conclusion. In principle, processes work through logically to their conclusion, rather like scientific method. In fact, processes, like scientific method, are often coloured by emotion – particularly where they involve advocacy or are avoiding unpalatable outcomes. If the premise, on which a process is based, is flawed the outcome may be perverse. Hitler was an extreme example of distorted logic and many people are skilled at diverting processes through selective distortion of the data involved or of the process steps themselves. Processes are essential tools of management but corporate governance needs to be alert to the danger of their abuse – not least in the finance area!

The importance of processes in managing enterprises is reflected in the focus on process in regulating them. External regulators are primarily concerned with ensuring market stability and competition; internal regulation is concerned with ensuring control. Both internal and external regulation require that players in the market place are financially sound and that their processes are effective in keeping them so. Most sizeable companies monitor their processes through internal audit and through assessment by their external auditor. A series of audit failures in recent years (WorldCom, Tyco, and so on) has raised concerns about the working of the relatively deregulated economy in the USA and UK. The use of codes for corporate governance is seeking to meet such concerns, not least in calling for certification of risk management controls (Turnbull Report). External regulation is contingent for most companies – the DTI has powers of inspection which may be used if required. Banks and most other financial services companies are subject to regulation by the Financial Services Authority; most utilities are also subject to pricing regulation.

One of the insidious pressures on processes is the practice of setting short-term targets for performance. At the extreme this can lead to massive subversion of processes, as with the destruction of Barings by Nick Leeson, and routinely leads to cheating (market timing, trading out of limits, and so on). British and Commonwealth was destroyed by salesmen who made unauthorised sale or return deals to build up their commission. For many years it was common practice to sell excess stock to outside firms at year end and to buy it back when stock had been taken and inventory levels reduced. Incentives which motivate employees to suborn processes for their own ends are self defeating. Where targets are based on longer-term results there is less incentive to cheat and time makes cheating difficult. Incentives which are based on long-term overall results for the company are less disruptive and invidious and, because they are not encouraging individuals to cheat, become self-policing.

BRAND

Through strong leadership in shaping an inclusive values-based culture, supported by the creation of an appropriate structure and processes to deliver consistent results, a company will build confidence and trust both inside and outside its ambit. Confidence and trust are the building blocks of reputation which is usually encapsulated in a company brand and/or a series of product brands.

A strong brand is built up over years and consistent corporate governance is required to build the trust on which it is founded. One of the key tasks of corporate governance is to develop and sustain behaviours which reflect the values espoused by the company. Such consistent behaviours are the building blocks of the company's reputation of which the brand is the external symbol.

The question of reputation is examined in detail in Chapter 8. We now need to address the interplay of values and behaviours and its impact on delivering effective corporate governance. It is in the interaction of people that companies achieve their purpose and that interaction needs to be shaped by shared values to produce consistent behaviours and sustained results. To achieve this we need to activate our basic model.

Activating the basic model of corporate governance

We have seen that the board has the fundamental responsibility for directing the company and for ensuring that it can be sustainably profitable. While the prime leadership for this process must come from the board in order to balance internal and external responsibilities, there is a need for the board's leadership to be echoed in all parts of the company and for all involved with the company, both employees and stakeholders, to contribute to sustaining that leadership. What needs to be done to activate and sustain our basic model? Let us examine this task under the headings used to shape our basic model:

1 Leadership
2 Culture
3 Structure
4 Processes
5 Brand.

In doing so we shall need to consider the internal structure of the company and the role of external stakeholders in achieving the company's purpose.

LEADERSHIP

All employees have potential for leadership since everybody has some talent in which they are outstanding. Some people are natural organisers, and head special interest groups; others are communicators and can influence their peers. It is interesting to watch a group of enthusiasts, seeing one person emerge to present on a specific topic in which he or she has expertise and then passing the lead to a colleague with a different agenda and set of skills. Most people enjoy taking leadership where they are equipped and motivated to do so – too few companies are willing or able to use this wealth of talent.

For some years many businesses have used multi-disciplinary teams to manage projects. Leadership in such teams moves to deal with specific specialisms as need arises, while the total project remains under the control of the project manager. This process is often compared to the performance of a symphony orchestra, where key solo parts bring out individual skills, yet the whole performance is integrated by the conductor.

Teamwork has been greatly facilitated by the development of the Internet, in particular by the use of in-house 'intranets' which improve the flow and exchange of knowledge and the communication of ideas. The use of 'chat rooms' can be a powerful means of building team collaboration and accelerating the completion of projects. This approach was used by Pfizer to accelerate the process of approving new medicines and it facilitates the interchange of ideas and the exchange of leadership between team members which drives the project to completion.

Workshops are another effective tool for helping teams to explore the issues which they need to resolve in order to make progress with a project. When workshops are facilitated to draw out ideas and stimulate open debate they can encourage teams to 'think the unthinkable' and can enable participants to take leadership in areas where their knowledge and experience are at a premium. One of the approaches to change management which has proved successful is to 'cascade' the process of debating and winning support for change down through an organisation by means of a series of structured workshops. Not only does this approach build ownership of change but it releases the leadership potential of those who will make it happen.

CULTURE

We have seen that the board has a basic responsibility for shaping the culture of the company it directs. This it does by defining the mission of the business and the values which it should espouse in order to fulfil that mission. All too often these are defined in a vacuum – they exist on paper or on the walls but do not shape the daily conduct of the company. Values can only be expressed through behaviours and those behaviours need to be consistent throughout the company if it is to build a distinctive culture.

One approach to testing the consistency between espoused values and actual behaviours has been developed by Gerard International Limited, an ethics consultancy. This involves a two-stage process: firstly, to ask participants to map their ideal pattern of behaviours against a grid of 14 value sets and seven rating levels (this is done without attribution) and secondly to play the game 'Dilemma!' in order to clarify their reaction to a series of 'real life' situations. This process is described in detail, with a typical case study, in Appendix B.

We have seen in Chapter 3 the importance of reputation, and how to develop and protect it. Any model for embedding good corporate governance into an organisation needs to address the building of sustainable reputation, and encapsulate it into a brand which its customers prefer. Reputation is based on consistent and predictable behaviours so that work done to align behaviours with espoused values, such as using techniques similar to that of Gerard International (see above), has to be reinforced by the total pattern of culture in the organisation. This requires all employees, in particular directors and other possible 'role models', to conform consistently to the values of the organisation. The main sign of success is when all employees see themselves as 'Cadbury' people, identifying themselves with the distinctive culture of their company. This is much more than wearing an uniform (though that may help in some cases); it is pride in belonging to a company which outsiders admire and consciousness of the need to maintain its reputation through their own conduct.

Companies which have an outstanding reputation can usually be very selective in their recruitment. New graduates want to work for BP or Unilever rather than for less illustrious and demanding employers. Creating a strong culture and ensuring that it is enhanced, never weakened, makes the company a magnet for recruiting the best talent. Some candidates for jobs are very mercenary and will never be more than a 'hired hand' while they seek a more highly paid job. These are not the people who build sustainable reputations but, if properly controlled, they may add value to the company as they focus on lining their pockets. What really matters is the reputation of the company – the 'star' system in the City can be very damaging, especially when internal emails are revealed (Henry Blodget and others). Wise companies recruit all personality types (as in Belbin or Myers-Briggs) in order to foster creative interaction between them. Recruiting clones of the present leaders perpetuates the past and impedes the ability of the company to change into the future. Companies are microcosms of society and need to foster diversity in recruitment in order to test and renew their culture. This does not mean that companies need to reflect the deviancy of society – it is the superior performance of excellent companies which pays the government to cope with the problems of society.

Culture in an organisation needs to reflect its purpose and priorities. The regime of an army is strict to reflect its need to provide effective defence. The purpose of most companies is to generate wealth primarily for its shareholders but also for the stakeholders who support its success. It will fulfil this purpose through its mission (the markets it serves and the products and services it offers) but its primary focus is on profitability. This means that the culture of a successful company must be businesslike and efficient. Wise companies create a culture which is open and friendly but which offers and expects respect between different parties in business dealings. Building relationships with such parties is part of good corporate governance.

A core function of culture is to determine the system of rewards and sanctions for motivating employees. This issue has become one of the *causes célèbres* of corporate governance, due to examples of manifest greed and inequity in the payment of directors which have been well publicised. This issue reflects the market manipulation practised by a number of executive directors, often with support from executive directors of other companies who sit as non-executive directors on their Remuneration Committee. Counter-ing this dominance of many boards by executive directors is a key part of the agenda of the Higgs Committee, and pressure continues to keep executive remuneration in proportion to that of other employees. A culture of greed is divisive and rarely sustainable, often because it is not balanced by effective sanctions. Boards need to be alert to the corrosive effects of greed, and shareholders need to be more active in preventing the plunder of their company, as happened most recently at Sainsbury's. Rewards must be geared to achieving company objectives, and must be proportionate to the returns to shareholders and other stakeholders to be sustainable.

Culture reflects the way that human beings interact and is shaped by the purpose of that interaction. In the same way that a market place is the sum of all the transactions which take place within its boarders, a culture is shaped by all the human relationships which take place both inside and outside an organisation in pursuit of its purpose. An entrepreneurial culture will attract creative and unconventional people – the advertising industry is a good example. The operators of 'hedge funds' are more daring and idiosyncratic than conventional fund managers. At the other extreme, civil servants operate within a set of formal and informal constraints, set by their political masters and precedent, which makes their culture defensive and conformist. For most businesses culture acts as a day-to-day touchstone for relationships and decision making – it is invisible but all pervasive.

STRUCTURE

The structure of the human body is largely inert, being bone for the most part, but the human skeleton is the essential platform for supporting the organs and processes which give us life. In the same way the structure of a company has to support its operations and processes but it also needs to provide a road map to guide them.

The rigidity and density of structure in an organisation will vary according to its nature. The civil service traditionally has a rigid and formalised structure in order to meet the demands of government for accountability. Civil servants are required to deliver government policy to citizens in a consistent and predictable manner. This requires a formal and dense structure to meet variable demand on a fixed basis. At the other extreme lie 'virtual' organisations which have little or no structure, in the sense of buildings or organisation charts, but can build teams to meet opportunities as they occur. The growth of the Internet has facilitated the creation and operation of virtual organisations, such as SAMI Consulting, a consultancy linked to St Andrews University which consists of a college of independent Fellows who form ad hoc teams to work with clients.

For most businesses, structure comprises a location, or group of locations, from which employees work in structured groups (divisions, departments, branches, and so on). Structure enables outsiders to find the business and the business to deal with them effectively. Structure needs to be locatable and able to respond to the needs of clients and others. Some businesses, for example, travel agencies and insurance brokers, have developed trading by telephone and on the Internet rather than through physical branches; this trend away from branches seems to have stalled as businesses find that many clients like to deal with a human person. Most businesses now treat telephone and Internet links as an alternative distribution channel to physical branches.

The implications of structure for corporate governance are considerable. Structure supports a company's operations and processes and needs sufficient strength to do so. Highly capitalised and process-intensive companies typically need a more robust structure than knowledge-based businesses, although the latter depend on sophisticated IT systems. One key issue of corporate governance is to protect the company infrastructure from fraud or external attack, for example, by hackers. Seemingly well-structured groups like Parmalat can be destroyed from inside by fraud; damage by hackers is usually hidden by companies so that the depredations of hackers are almost certainly under recorded. Effective implementation of the Turnbull Report recommendations is probably a key approach to protecting structure but this will require greater imagination and foresight than most organisations commit to this task if structure is to be well protected. For any organisation it is essential to plan for disaster recovery, for example after a fire; this helps to clarify the best means of protecting its structure in the first place.

PROCESSES

If protecting structure is of great importance to an organisation, the development and nurture of processes is its very lifeblood. Even virtual organisations are animated by processes. What are the governance issues faced by organisations in respect of processes?

The first key issue is to ensure that processes are 'fit for purpose'. Too often processes are copied from elsewhere without a fundamental assessment of their purpose and whether they can achieve it. Too many consultants offer generic processes and fail to adapt them to the needs of their clients. Like computer programmes, processes can be adapted for purpose or can be tailor-made. Tailored processes are usually more expensive but if well designed can be more efficient, easier to use and accommodate change with greater facility. Process design and control is a key function of any business but too many companies leave it to consultants to install their processes and fail to achieve 'fitness for purpose'. Because they have not thought through the functions of their processes they also fail to gain the understanding to be able to protect and modify them effectively. Organisations should treat processes as a key dimension of their Turnbull reporting and develop in-house competence in their design and maintenance.

It is maintenance which is the second key governance issue for companies. Processes are living things and require constant attention and care. The importance of processes was recognised in the work done on work-study by Taylor and others in the early twentieth century, initially on factory processes and later on clerical operations. Work-study not only sought to improve productivity but acted to protect the integrity of the new processes it developed. With the growth of computing and of dispersed operations some of the rigour of the earlier work-study ethos has been lost in many organisations. Once again the Turnbull reporting requirement offers the opportunity of winning back control of internal processes.

The need to nurture and protect processes is enhanced by the dangers of 'open computing' which increase the risk of contamination by viruses and 'worms'. It is also increased by the growing activity of 'hackers', both for criminal and disruptive purposes. Such activity damages both records, on which processes depend, and often processes themselves. Most organisations rely on internal audits to find and rectify damage to their processes; good governance requires a more proactive approach of building robust processes, protecting them against likely dangers and adapting them to meet changing circumstances. If this work is linked to a search for continuous productivity improvements, it can justify the creation of a new model of 'organisation and methods' function, reverting to Taylorian principles but operating in a fast-changing modern context. Such an approach would be a significant advance on building productivity through 'downsizing'. It would build productivity by enhancing internal control.

BRAND

Building brand values is a long-term undertaking and requires sustained commitment. Provided that a company's corporate governance system is sound and focused on the longer term, it is likely that confidence and trust between all stakeholders will grow and that the reputation of the company will grow in tandem with them. Converting that good reputation into a brand which commands preference in the market place does, however, require further specific action.

Traditionally the development and exploitation of brands have been seen as a marketing responsibility. Consequently the focus of brand promotion has been on consumers, both to develop brand recognition and then create brand preference. As a result many companies have concentrated on product brands, for example, Lipton, rather than corporate brands (Unilever). Consumers recognise Johnny Walker rather than Diageo. Other companies have merged their product brands behind their corporate brand, for example, Nestlé. The link between product brands and corporate governance is often tenuous. It is in part to counter this that Unilever has reduced its brand portfolio from 1600 to 400 and is seeking greater recognition of its corporate brand.

Increasing demands for public accountability are driving the growth of corporate brands. Consumers are now more sophisticated and can recognise the link between Dove soap and Unilever. Nestlé continues to be linked with the local difficulties associated with its baby milk powder. In markets which are increasingly competitive, consumers will only grant a brand premium to products which are backed by world-class companies. Consumers are also more sensitive to the behaviour of these companies in world markets as with Nike and child labour in the Third World.

Many companies see branding as an output of their corporate governance activities rather than as a driver of better governance. A few such as BP have used corporate governance to differentiate themselves from their competitors. BP has emphasised corporate social responsibility as a key feature to distinguish itself from Exxon Mobil. Diageo has focused on corporate governance (see Chapter 5) in order to build brand values which distinguish it from other groups in the alcoholic drinks business. Most companies, however, are less concerned to be outstanding in the FTSE4 Good Index than to create shareholder value. Many such companies see corporate governance as an external hurdle to jump rather than a way of life which builds shareholder value through the trust of stakeholders. Many such companies live in fear of the next revelation which undermines their brand value. After Shell, who is next?

How should companies use their brand equity to reinforce corporate governance? BP has shown a way to do this, by changing its corporate logo and projecting the image of a company 'beyond petroleum' while confirming and reinforcing its brand values in a new context. Greater emphasis on corporate social responsibility backed by 'state of the art' corporate governance seeks to put BP in a category beyond that in which its peers are left behind. BP is seeking to create a super brand which is sustained by a peerless reputation among all who deal with it. Few companies can generate sufficient trust in the market place to emulate BP, which enjoys a reputation for building shareholder value and for social responsibility. Oil companies are vulnerable in environmental issues (and some on ethical trading) but BP has enjoyed a 'teflon' image to date. A profile of the BP which emerged from the multiple mergers of the 1990s, may be found in Chapter 5.

One novel approach to building brand equity may emerge from C. K. Pralahad's new book, *The Fortune at the Bottom of the Pyramid: Eradicating Poverty through Profits* (Wharton School, 2004). This recommends that businesses should focus not on a limited population of wealthy people but on the mass of potential consumers at the 'bottom of the pyramid'. This requires a whole new mindset; products need to be developed which will meet the needs of poor people who wish to begin to consume. For years Unilever has sold shampoo in single sachets; the 'bottom of the pyramid' market is for tiny unit sales in huge quantities (much as Woolworth pioneered before the Second World War in its '3d and 6d' stores). Organising the development of such a market is an enormous task and bureaucracy and corruption will need to be overcome as well as the scepticism of poor consumers. If they can be made to believe that they are taken seriously as customers, and can begin to live as entrepreneurs rather than victims, the goodwill generated will represent brand value on a scale never before achieved.

Integrating the corporate governance model

We have examined the implementation of corporate governance in a number of key dimensions. All of these need to be subjected to the process of governance but their interaction needs to be integrated with rigour in order to make the total system effective. The system should also be subject to independent review at regular intervals to ensure that it meets or beats best practice.

Many companies have made special arrangements in order to be able to report their performance against the Combined Code and in respect of public expectations of their social and environmental accountability. Some, like Diageo, have taken a 'compliance' approach, seeking to change attitudes and behaviours initially through meeting standards, with the intention of creating over time a culture which breeds trust and co-operation. Such an approach needs to address both internal constituencies and external parties which interact with the company. See Chapter 5 for details of Diageo's system.

Other companies have taken an approach which focuses on all stakeholders in the business and actively builds relationships with them. This approach was pioneered in the UK by British Telecom, which created the post of Director of Corporate Governance to spearhead progress (see my *A Strategic Approach to Corporate Governance*, p. 169ff). This initiative has now developed into a programme to create stakeholder value through corporate social responsibility. Another stakeholder-focused approach was pioneered by Sir John Egan when chairman of BAA in order to win acceptance for the expansion of Heathrow Airport. This is well described in his book (with Des Wilson) *Private Business – Public Battleground* (Palgrave, 2002). The stakeholder value model was created by Johnson & Johnson, through the rigorous use of the 'credo' or values statement penned by Robert Wood Johnson, who led the company from 1938 to 1963. The 'credo' has now become embedded in the daily operations of the company and is the touchstone for all decisions in its large and decentralised business. A copy of the 'credo' is shown in Appendix C. It is interesting that Sir John Egan always tests his major decisions against the mission statement of his company. Both approaches ensure consistency and predictability.

ALLOCATING POWER

Organisations work through the allocation of power. In many smaller companies power is concentrated, often in the hands of one person, and is delegated only to the extent which is required in any given situation. Lack of empowerment makes it difficult to recruit talent into such companies so that their ability to grow (and even survive) is circumscribed and contingent on events. This constraint is one of the reasons for the slow decline in the numbers of family companies and for the dramatic failure of big ones like WorldCom and Vivendi which were dominated by individuals.

In an increasingly competitive and changing world most companies now see the need to devolve power to the areas from which profits and growth are derived. Most operational decisions need to be made quickly and seldom put the business at risk. Many strategic decisions can be delegated to executives who are informed of corporate strategy and can test them against that strategy. By devolving power and negotiating clear limits to the authority of those empowered most businesses can harness the initiative and skills of key staff to grow market share and profits. This process needs to be underpinned by shared values in order to ensure a consistency of behaviours and concern for the welfare of the enterprise.

The directors of a company are responsible for its direction and therefore hold the power needed for that task. They are responsible primarily to the company and answerable to its shareholders. In modern thinking they are not simple agents of the shareholders otherwise they would need permission for every action – *delegatus non potest delegare* (agents cannot delegate their powers). They have the power to act as they deem fit, but remain accountable to the owners of the company. As a result the power they give to others is for the benefit of the company but not limited except where express provisions are made. This ability to act except where specifically constrained is the difference between empowerment and licence. Empowerment can release creative and dynamic forces which licence constrains, yet it is empowerment which has made the dramatic growth of the modern economy possible. Empowerment does, however, rely on the integrity and human qualities of those who receive it. Recurrent business scandals remind us of the need to empower with care and to support those whom we have empowered. The case study on The Carphone Warehouse (Chapter 5) shows the dramatic results achievable through empowerment.

DEVELOPING THE CORPORATE GOVERNANCE SYSTEM

In too many companies corporate governance is seen as an exercise carried out to satisfy the Stock Exchange and shareholders who wish to ensure that codes are respected in order to preserve share value. Many companies use corporate governance as a vehicle for public relations and issue special reports on their commitment to social and environmental responsibility. Enron was exemplary in its corporate governance reporting but this, as we now know, was nothing but a 'whited sepulchre'.

The observation of the Combined Code is only the first step in implementing corporate governance. Full implementation can only be achieved by involving all parts of the company and external stakeholders who operate in its wider ambit. To do this the corporate governance system must be as all-pervading as the management system is expected to be. It needs to be supported by comprehensive training to ensure consistency. The corporate governance system has to be at the heart of strategy and operations, not a veneer to cover their inadequacy. Few companies have made any significant progress towards achieving this.

How can a company create a system to take corporate governance beyond the boardroom into the whole of its zone of influence? Even within the ambit of the company itself obedience is not unqualified; with external stakeholders co-operation has to be negotiated. At one level, compliance with a company's regime of governance can be bought yet this conflicts with the fundamental principle of paying for economic benefits. Even where compliance produces financial rewards they cannot outweigh the rewards due for economic success without creating confusion. Being nice is not as important in business as making profits.

Business involves co-operation in order to achieve results. The fruits of these results can be shared on an agreed basis. Without co-operation there are unlikely to be fruits to share; it is something other than just the hope of profits which engenders and sustains co-operation. I believe that for most people this is a shared set of values which builds the trust needed for co-operation. Values are the currency which sustains any successful system of corporate governance.

VALUES

We have explored ethics and principles in earlier chapters and seen how they are at the core of human relationships and thus of corporate governance as well. We have seen how companies define their purpose in mission statements and usually define at the same time the values they expect their colleagues to espouse in fulfilling the mission statement. Johnson & Johnson's 'credo' (see Appendix C) combines both mission and values. Some companies such as Morrisons Supermarkets have homely values and a blunt mission:

- *Our philosophy is to offer outstanding value for money, unbeatable customer service and a pleasant shopping experience.*
- *We are renowned for our 'no nonsense' approach to retailing, shunning hype and gimmicks in favour of plain selling. We are consistent and reliable in offering honest, good value.*
- *It is 'Morrison's Mission' to always deliver – 'The Very Best for Less'.*

Other companies have more extensive values. The values of General Motors are shown in Exhibit 1 and lack the focus of those of Morrison. The values of 3M (Exhibit 2) are more of a sales prospectus than a set of values. One set of values which have a community as well as a business dimension is that of The Home Depot (Exhibit 3). Lockheed Martin has a corporate value statement, 'Setting the Standard', which is aspirational in tone and focused on the human relationships which make business successful (Exhibit 4). It is noteworthy that the leading value is 'ethics', setting the tone for the rest of the values and making them much more than a 'sales pitch'. Having examined these and a considerable number of other values statements, I find that the Johnson & Johnson 'credo' remains the most compelling. It is also one which has been severely tested by the Tylenol crises of 1982 and 1986 when the

EXHIBIT 1: GM – GMABILITY COMMUNITY INVOLVEMENT: CORE GM VALUES

GM has defined six core values for the conduct of its business:

- Continuous improvement
- Customer enthusiasm
- Innovation
- Integrity
- Teamwork
- Individual respect and responsibility.

These values are the basis upon which all GM employees conduct their day-to-day business, and are the foundation of GM's guidelines for employee conduct, Winning With Integrity, Our Values and Guidelines for Employee Conduct. These guidelines, which demonstrate GM's commitment to integrity, include personal integrity, integrity in the workplace, integrity in the marketplace, and integrity in society and its communities.

In May 1999, GM announced its support of the Global Sullivan Principles as being consistent with GM's internal policies and principles, including its Winning With Integrity guidelines. The Global Sullivan Principles, which were developed by the Reverend Leon H. Sullivan and have their roots in the 1977 Sullivan Principles for South Africa, provide guidance to companies across the globe regarding core issues such as human rights, worker rights, the environment, community relations, supplier relations and fair competition.

CORPORATE VALUES AND SUSTAINABILITY

3M's sustainability policies and practices are directly linked to our four fundamental corporate values:

- Satisfying our customers with superior quality and value

- Providing investors an attractive return through sustained, high-quality growth

- Respecting our social and physical environment

- Being a company that employees are proud to be part of.

THE HOME DEPOT VALUES

Associates are central to Home Depot's success and our values are part of the fabric of the company. Values are beliefs that do not change over time. They are what we believe in, what we do, and what govern our decisions on a day-to-day basis. They are the principles and standards for the framework upon which Home Depot is built. Home Depot's unique culture is built on associate dedication and a commitment to an 'orange-blooded' entrepreneurial spirit.

1 *Taking care of our people:* The key to our success is treating people well. We do this by encouraging associates to speak up and take risks, by recognizing and rewarding good performance and by leading and developing people so they may grow.

2 *Giving back to our communities:* An important part of the fabric of The Home Depot is giving our time, talents, energy and resources to worthwhile causes in our communities and society.

3 *Doing the right thing:* We exercise good judgement by 'doing the right thing' instead of just 'doing things right'. We strive to understand the impact of our decisions, and we accept responsibility for our actions.

4 *Excellent customer service:* Along with our quality products, service, price and selection, we must go the extra mile to give customers knowledgeable advice about merchandise and to help them use those products to their maximum benefit.

5 *Creating shareholder value:* The investors who provide the capital necessary to allow our company to grow need and expect a return on their investment. We are committed to providing it.

6 *Building strong relationships:* Strong relationships are built on trust, honesty and integrity. We listen and respond to the needs of customers, associates, communities and vendors, treating them as partners.

7 *Entrepreneurial spirit:* Home Depot associates are encouraged to initiate creative and innovative ways of serving our customers and improving the business and to spread best practices throughout the company.

8 *Respect for all people:* In order to remain successful, our associates must work in an environment of mutual respect, free of discrimination and harassment where each associate is regarded as a part of The Home Depot team.

EXHIBIT 4: LOCKHEED MARTIN

CORPORATE VALUE STATEMENT

Our Value Statement – 'Setting the Standard'

These are the standards that inform and inspire all of our activities, and distinguish us as a corporation.

- Ethics
- Excellence
- 'Can-do'
- Integrity
- People
- Teamwork.

Ethics   We will be well-informed in the regulations, rules and compliance issues that apply to our businesses around the world. We will apply this knowledge to our conduct as responsible employees of Lockheed Martin, and will adhere to the highest standards of ethical conduct in all that we do.

Excellence   The pursuit of superior performance infuses every Lockheed Martin activity. We excel at meeting challenging commitments even as we achieve total customer satisfaction. We demonstrate leadership by advancing new technologies, innovative manufacturing techniques, enhanced customer service, inspired management, and the application of best practices throughout our organisation. Each of us leads through our individual contributions to Lockheed Martin's core purpose.

'Can-do'   We demonstrate individual leadership through a positive approach to every task, a 'can-do' spirit, and a restless determination to continually improve upon our personal bests. We aggressively pursue new business, determined to add value for our customers with ingenuity, determination and a positive attitude. We utilise our ability to combine strength with speed in responding enthusiastically to every new opportunity and every new challenge.

Integrity   Each of us brings to the workplace personal values which guide us to meet our commitments to customers, suppliers, colleagues, and others with whom we interact. We embrace truthfulness and trust, and we treat everyone with dignity and respect – as we wish to be treated ourselves.

People   Outstanding people make Lockheed Martin unique. Success in rapidly changing markets requires that we continuously learn and grow as individuals and as an organisation. We embrace lifelong learning through individual initiative, combined with company-sponsored education and development programmes, as well as challenging work and growth opportunities.

Teamwork   We multiply the creativity, talents and contributions of both individuals and businesses by focusing on team goals. Our teams assume collective accountability for their actions, share trust and leadership, embrace diversity, and accept responsibility for prudent risk taking. Each of us succeeds individually … when we as a team achieve success.

product was adulterated with cyanide for use as a murder weapon. By clearing the stock from all shelves and facing the situation regardless of cost, Johnson & Johnson was able to preserve its reputation into the future.

STAKEHOLDERS

Companies engage with many stakeholders on a commercial basis; with key stakeholders they need to build human relationships. One of the key tasks in corporate governance is to identify and rank stakeholders in terms of their importance to the company's business. It is often useful to map stakeholders in their relationship to the company and to capture any cross-relationships between them and non-stakeholders such as competitors, media, and so on. This helps to understand the strength of the relationship between each stakeholder and the company. The map should also allow potential relationships to be identified, for example, a competitor in one market may be an ideal partner in another context. For example, BAE SYSTEMS and Thales are intense competitors yet they are partners in building the new aircraft carrier for the Royal Navy.

The complexities of modern life are making for more flexible relationships. Companies increasingly need to share supply chains in order to obtain economies of scale and maximum efficiency. Logistics companies have to handle the trade secrets of multiple competitors every day and deal with their clients even-handedly. Business relationships are not only becoming more complex, they are also increasingly volatile. As a result companies need to give relationships more intensive and continuous attention. Marketing departments have for years had account managers; other key relationships need the same personal involvement to be successful. A supply chain is not only a series of important links, it is a living thing which changes to meet changing circumstances and in which all participants need to work and co-operate harder than ever to make it competitive.

This concept of collaboration has been developed into a total system by the Voluntary Interindustry Commerce Standards Association. This is entitled 'Collaborative Planning, Forecasting and Replenishment' and involves companies such as Wal-Mart, Lucent Technologies, Sara Lee, Warner Lambert and SAP. It has developed a number of process models which:

- are open but allow secure communications;
- are flexible across the industry;
- are extensible to all supply chain processes; and
- support a broad set of requirements (inter-operability, new data types, and so on).

Similar supply chain co-operatives have been formed for specific retail industries such as groceries, to cover an international spectrum. Most participants are using such vehicles for generic lines of business; more specific products may not be suitable for a co-operative supply chain and trust needs to be developed before key business lines are included.

Co-operative enterprise works in other ways. The Manufacturing Extension Partnership is a network of advisory centres which work with US smaller manufacturers on a not-for-profit basis to solve a wide range of problems. In the UK the Department of Trade and Industry (DTI) provides a number of similar services. The co-operative approach facilitates learning and builds relationships for the future. There are a myriad of service offers on the Internet which are not quality controlled and may not be appropriate for many companies to use. Co-operative or 'club' facilities are likely to develop partnerships through working together, rather than models conceived by external consultants.

It is useful to explore new avenues, such as those mentioned above, in order to extend the stakeholder network of the company and build its knowledge bank. Stakeholder relations are precious but companies need to keep them under constant review and introduce new relationships and abandon stale relationships in order to sustain and develop their business.

REPUTATION MANAGEMENT

We have seen earlier (Chapter 3) the importance of building and maintaining the reputation of the company. We have also examined brand management earlier in this chapter. All employees and stakeholders are involved in building and maintaining the company's reputation so that the process of doing so needs to be integrated into the corporate governance system of the company. This may be done in several ways:

- By focusing on reputational risk issues in reporting against the Turnbull Report requirements.
- By establishing and monitoring an agreed set of values for use in all relationships both inside and outside the company (see above).
- By aligning all reward systems to group objectives primarily, and to personal achievement secondarily (see Culture above).
- By distilling out of all work on reputation management a quintessence which can be projected and nurtured as a brand (see above).

Responsibility for reputation management lies with the board and the issue should be reviewed regularly. Most boards delegate the detailed work to a nominated official, frequently the company secretary or the director of corporate governance (if there is one). Such delegation does not absolve the directors from personal responsibility in protecting and building the company's reputation.

Reputation management may be approached as a compliance issue (to meet Turnbull requirements) with an emphasis on preventing or dealing with crises, litigation, complaints and media criticisms. This approach handles negative situations but does little to create positive effects. Reputation management should be focused on building and sustaining a better reputation and benchmarking the company against the best exemplars. Many companies follow *Fortune* ratings of 'The Global Most Admired Companies', 'The 100 Best Companies to Work For' and 'America's Most Admired Companies' (www.fortune.com). There are many sources of advice, including 'The Reputation Institute' (www.reputationinstitute.com), MORI Research (www.mori.com), 'Harris Interactive' (www.harrisinteractive.com) and Manchester Business School Corporate Reputation Institute (www.mbs.ac.uk). Other sources include major consulting firms and insurance brokers, such as Aon and Jardine Lloyd Thompson. To create a method of rating it is necessary to identify the components of reputation in the sector served by the company (quality, service, innovation, staff attitudes, and so on) and their relative proportions. The best company in the sector can be rated accordingly and this sets an initial benchmark for the company to achieve. Ratings should be done by an independent party such as MORI so that they are consistent and unbiased. It is also useful to have an independent survey of customers and prospective customers to determine what features they would like to have which are not currently on offer. This will help to shape the company and its ratings in a more competitive direction. I wonder whether clients would have voted for the call centres which cause such frustration and destroy goodwill?

A study by Fombrun, Gardberg and Sever (2000) in the *Journal of Brand Management* (7(4), pp. 241–55) identified the following key reputation attributes (through focus groups):

- Familiarity   Knowing the companies or its products well.
- Creating value   Producing high-quality products, providing value for money.
- Operational capability   Being well-run, efficient and productive.
- Corporate citizenship   Caring about its employees/the community.
- Performance   Proven track record, good use of assets.
- Leadership/management   Having a CEO with vision, communicating values.
- Appeal   Being liked by stakeholders, being a good company to work for.
- Credibility   Being trustworthy, standing behind its practices.

It is interesting that being 'easy to work with' was not emphasised – perhaps disillusionment with call centres came after 2000! Although these attributes are not surprising, they provide a basis for rating a company, although it may also be useful to find attributes which were not mentioned and were not expected. Developing some of these, such as innovation, may add a competitive edge to the company. Some companies such as 3M and Reckitt Benckiser are driven by innovation. Given the importance of reputation management, I have sought the views of Stewart Lewis, Head of MORI's Reputation Centre, which has been a trail blazer in this area (see Chapter 7).

Summary

We have explored how to set up a corporate governance system and how it should be managed to reach all parts of a company's zone of operation and the stakeholders within it. Such a system has a number of key imperatives:

- The full and continuing support of the board and its relevant committees (audit in particular).
- The nomination of a senior executive to drive and control the system (company secretary, corporate governance director, compliance director, and so on).
- Independent advice on best practice and, ideally, a regular independent review of the working of the system.
- Reporting lines have to be established. At present most companies report governance matters through the Audit Committee (which is a rather defensive posture). The creation of a Corporate Governance Committee of the board is likely to be a better way to emphasise the use of corporate governance to win competitive advantage (see above).
- The corporate governance function and its leader need to be at the heart of intra and extra company communications in order to receive full feedback.
- The corporate governance function should have a primary responsibility for liaison with all stakeholders in the company and integrating policy towards them and their interactivity with the company. This does not inhibit normal commercial relationships but ensures that stakeholders have a holistic relationship with the company and 'feel part of the family'.
- One of the key functions of the people working the system is to train staff and selected stakeholders in the requirements of the system. New employees need to understand quickly what is expected of them. The system needs to cope with part-time and interim workers and with outworking contracts.

- Values need to be agreed, monitored and regularly reviewed. All reward systems need to be geared to values, not just to short-term individual performance.
- The full support of all involved in or affected by the corporate government system is essential for success. All must be free to criticise its working and to 'blow the whistle' when it is threatened by malpractice.
- Finally, the system should serve to enhance the long-term success of the company, not create a self-serving bureaucracy.

REPORTING/FEEDBACK

The corporate governance model needs constantly to be adapted to meet new circumstances. To guide this adaptation the system needs to provide a steady stream of business intelligence, both in the form of regular reporting and through alert feedback from employees and stakeholders. Much of this intelligence will come from sales reports, market analysis, supplier evaluations, economic reports and other external sources, and will be primarily destined for use by operating departments. Through a company intranet such intelligence can be integrated for use in refining the corporate governance system. This intelligence is of such potential importance that it needs to be synthesised into regular reports to executive management and the board. The board is responsible for establishing and maintaining the corporate governance system and any changes to the system need to be formally approved by the board.

2 Different Models of Corporate Governance

We have been concerned to synthesise the essence of corporate governance and to examine how it may be taken from a top-level, compliance-orientated stance to become embedded in the daily routine of the organisation. Much has been written about the theory of corporate governance but the implementation of that theory, outside the routine of company reporting, remains largely unachieved. Behind the rhetoric of consultants and the bravura of conferences there is a *terra incognita* which few companies have really explored. There are some organisations which have been working to develop corporate governance and to move its boundaries out from the boardroom into the real world of business. The following case studies may help readers to see how they can make their corporate governance more effective and, hopefully, will encourage them to explore some new possibilities.

The case studies have been grouped for ease of understanding and comparison under the following headings:

- Specific companies (Chapter 5)
- Entrepreneurs and family companies (Chapter 6)
- Reputation and social and ecological responsibility (Chapter 7)
- Risk and investment (Chapter 8).

Where appropriate these case studies have been cross referenced to the main text of the book.

5 *Company Models*

These company models are taken both from large corporations and from smaller, entrepreneurial companies. The key feature of all case studies is their emphasis on people, rather than processes. They rely on open communication, empowerment and accountability. Each is a successful business and the case studies are intended to show how they use corporate governance to build the future of their company.

The Carphone Warehouse

A *Financial Times* supplement on 12 November 2003, entitled 'Understanding Entrepreneur-ship', draws a distinction between serial entrepreneurs and founder managers. Both are entrepreneurs, since both create new enterprises and commit themselves and their investors to risk, yet serial entrepreneurs seem to have a compulsion to repeat the agony and the ecstasy, whereas founder managers find fulfilment in nurturing and developing their sole creation. Many serial entrepreneurs, such as Richard Branson and Stelios Haji-Ioannou, find themselves destroying value in many new businesses and depending on a few key successes to fund their ambitions. Other entrepreneurs, such as Alan Leighton, find that 'going plural' enables them to further their ambitions from earnings as non-executive directors.

It is not easy to classify Charles Dunstone, the founder and chief executive of The Carphone Warehouse Group. Charles does not see himself as an entrepreneur but rather as a founder manager. With a background in the IT business, Charles was aware of the forces shaping the convergence of IT and telecoms, and of the long-term potential of mobile telephony, both for voice and data transmission. His particular insight was the recognition that mobile phones were both exciting and perplexing to potential users. With both manufacturers and service providers competing for control of the industry and creating conflicting messages for consumers, Charles saw the need for an independent and reliable source of advice for potential users of mobile phones. The Carphone Warehouse was seen not as a pure distributor but as the source of the widest range of choice and as an informed 'sounding board' in making a decision to buy. The model is not dissimilar to the ideal role of the independent financial adviser (IFA) in the financial services sector – unfortunately too few IFAs have maintained a consistent level of integrity over the years.

Integrity is at the heart of the operations of The Carphone Warehouse. If it is to be more than a 'middleman', the company has to build trust, primarily among potential mobile phone users, but also among suppliers and service providers. To do so it needs to build a cadre of employees, which is expert in the possibilities and trade-offs of mobile telephony, but committed to the company values. Its in-store staff are identified as consultants, not sales people. Their role is to provide understanding and advice – at The Carphone Warehouse products and services are bought, not sold.

In order to ensure that the pattern of integrity is maintained across a growing network of outlets in different areas, both in the UK and overseas, The Carphone Warehouse has developed a three-stage process for growing its cadre of consultants. Recruitment is a key process and focuses on well-qualified and highly motivated people from all sectors of society. Diversity is both desirable in itself but also to match the diversity of customers. By offering above average salaries and a clear career development path, The Carphone Warehouse attracts ambitious and intelligent recruits. It has a higher proportion of graduate staff than any other retail business. Recruitment is also driven by local shops, enabling local staff to meet candidates and ensuring that local teams maintain their cohesion.

The second focus of the process is training, which involves a full induction process in order to understand the philosophy and core practices of The Carphone Warehouse. Charles Dunstone has laid down five fundamental rules, which are at the heart of the business:

- If we don't look after the customer, someone else will.
- Nothing is gained by winning an argument but losing a customer.
- Always deliver what we promise. If in doubt under promise and over deliver.
- Always treat customers as we ourselves would like to be treated.
- The reputation of the whole company is in the hands of each individual.

This training is given both centrally and in the shop in which the new recruit will work. Training focuses on 'bringing the newcomer into the family' and on developing in him or her the behaviours which reflect the values of The Carphone Warehouse family. These values place the customer at the centre of all activities; Charles Dunstone is fanatical on the primacy of the customer, so that delighting customers is the key focus of the business of The Carphone Warehouse. Delighting customers, and encouraging them both to come back for further advice and to send their friends to experience 'The Carphone Warehouse effect', is the wellspring of the company's profits.

Training at The Carphone Warehouse focuses both on emotional intelligence and knowledge. Customers seek the best advice, and consultants are trained and motivated to have comprehensive and up-to-date knowledge of information technology and communications (ITC) equipment and its usage. Many go to great lengths to perfect and maintain their knowledge and are encouraged to do so. Some have become widely recognised as sources of independent and valuable advice. Their training also helps them to relate to a wide range of customers, of differing skills and ages, with consistency and confidence backed by a proprietary process 'Solve' which helps to mirror customers' real needs.

The third stage of developing consultants at The Carphone Warehouse is to empower them. Customers develop trust in the knowledge and behaviours of consultants, and empowering them enables the customer to complete a transaction with confidence once his or her mind is made up. Customers need to feel that they have both the best advice and the best deal. The Carphone Warehouse operates on the same 'never knowingly undersold' principle as John Lewis Group. Customers can be sure of having the best possible price and consultants are empowered to ensure that they receive it. This is often facilitated by the encouragement to shop managers to price tactically to meet local competition. Consultants are empowered to deal with the customer; they have no discretion with suppliers and may not participate in promotional deals, in case their independence and objectivity are put at risk. Charles Dunstone goes to great lengths to avoid supplier promotions towards individual consultants and to control group promotions carefully. All consultants are paid a good basic salary to avoid any temptation to favour any supplier.

The 1200 individual shops are the friendly and trusted face of The Carphone Warehouse towards its customers. They are directed and supported by the 'Support Centre', a way of putting 'Head Office' at the bottom of an inverted pyramid and emphasising the supremacy of customers and empowering those who serve them. This focus on customer interface has been adopted to the wholesale and fixed line businesses of The Carphone Warehouse and provides a palpable competitive edge. All support operations are run on 'lean and mean' principles so that resources are concentrated on the customer interface. The main Support Centre of the Carphone Warehouse is in North Acton Business Park in London and is focused on efficiency, not opulence. All offices are laid out in open plan and directors are located in 'goldfish bowls' run on 'open door' principles. Informality is reflected in behaviour everywhere in The Carphone Warehouse and all employees are able to email Charles Dunstone directly. When the company was floated on the Stock Exchange all employees were given shares, which many have retained. All managers have a share option scheme and employees have a 'Save as You Earn' scheme, linked to share options.

The focus of The Carphone Warehouse on mobile phones has been seen by some investors as too narrow. In fact the early move to seize the position of market arbiter has enabled the company to grow and evolve as the market for mobile phones has become more complex and increasingly driven by fashion. The Carphone Warehouse has become a key channel of communication between the ambitions of users and the research and development priorities of manufacturers. It is able to identify new market needs, for example, personal ring tones and new applications of mobile phones, such as photo exchange. The use of mobile phones for accessing the Internet, photography and downloading text are all developments which enrich customers' use of mobile phones and drive the demand for models with extra features. In time we may even see customers changing their mobile phones as readily as 'Swatches'!

The Carphone Warehouse recognises that consumers are ambitious and demanding and that their hunger for novelty and products to enhance their lifestyle will drive the mobile phone market. Few markets today are constrained by technology – innovation depends on creating demand and satisfying it rapidly and cheaply. Charles Dunstone understands the primacy of customers in business and goes to great lengths to communicate with them. Focus groups are a basic research tool for The Carphone Warehouse, supplemented by structured market surveys and by the daily feedback from its stores. Charles Dunstone is freely available to customers when necessary, but his policy of empowering his staff has made his intervention rarely required. His work for the Prince's Trust and other charities does more to build trust among the public than high-profile appearances and public relations activities. Few people know that he offers jobs in his call centres to homeless people and ex-servicemen, yet this is but a small part of the network of trust which sustains The Carphone Warehouse.

The Carphone Warehouse complies with both the Combined Code of Corporate Governance and the Turnbull Report. Its board comprises five executive and six non-executive directors, one of whom, Hans Snook, is chairman. Four of the non-executive directors are fully independent; Hans Snook has one million share options and Martin Dawes has a contingent interest in the future performance of Opal Telecom. Action will, therefore, be needed to restore a majority of fully independent non-executive directors on the board to meet the requirements of the Higgs Report. Action will also be necessary to ensure the rotation of auditor as required by the Smith Report. The senior non-executive director of The

Carphone Warehouse is Sir Brian Pitman who can be relied upon to meet both the letter and spirit of governance requirements.

What of the future? Charles Dunstone has moved skilfully to position The Carphone Warehouse in the wider telecoms industry by acquiring Opal Telecom plc, a provider of value-added fixed-line services. The company already has a well-established wholesale division which supports its retail business through bulk purchasing and disposal of used hand-sets, and handles support activities such as voucher distribution. The Carphone Warehouse is already an international business, retailing in France, Germany, Spain, the Netherlands and most major European countries, and it has an insurance business based in the Isle of Man and Switzerland. The growing complexity and cost of mobile ITC equipment may offer opportunities in financing deals, much as General Motors and General Electric have done with success for many years. The retail co-operation agreement with Sainsbury's may be the model for other similar 'in store' arrangements in the future. By owning the relationship with the customer on which all business is built, The Carphone Warehouse has positioned itself in the vanguard of business development. Like a skilful yachtsman, Charles Dunstone has taken the wind and now has to respond to its unpredictability.

POSTSCRIPT

Building on the success of The Carphone Warehouse, Charles Dunstone and his co-founder, David Ross, are making a gesture which extends the boundaries of corporate governance into new territory. Both have decided to give a large number of their company shares to some 40 key managers below board level; with a further contribution from another founder, Guy Johnstone, the gift totals five million shares. A three-year share option scheme for the company's 500 store managers has also been announced. The share gift is conditional on recipients remaining employed by the company on 1 October 2006, so that both schemes help to underpin the launch of 3G services and the market surge which it is expected to cause. Such schemes are also the cement for building teamwork – an essential foundation for good governance.

Cobra Beer

The key elements of corporate governance are to have clear objectives and the structure, procedures and culture to implement them. Karan Bilimoria has been focused on developing and promoting his unique formula for beer, and had the training at Ernst & Young to develop the tools to make it happen. He also learned about the presence of office politics, which can flourish where corporate objectives are subsumed in personal agendas. As an entrepreneur Karan is filled with enthusiasm for building Cobra Beer into an iconic brand but knows from experience that he has to transmit and sustain that enthusiasm to his colleagues in order to succeed. This he does by engaging them with a set of values, which are reflected in consistent behaviours and examples.

The values behind Cobra Beer derive from the motto of Karan's great grandfather 'aspire and achieve' – to which Karan has added 'against all odds'. The key value is passion, focused on a vision for the product, supported by commitment to all stakeholders (customers, employees, suppliers, local community) and integrity. Success is impossible without the passion to make others believe in the vision which drives you.

When Karan started Cobra Beer it was with a mission to produce a less gassy lager which would perfectly complement Indian food and appeal to fans of 'real ale'. In doing so he began an enterprise that had to challenge large established brewers. Karan had no brewer to produce his formula until he managed to persuade Dr Cariapa of Mysore Breweries to back his mission, to create and market the finest ever Indian beer. Only passion enabled Karan to convince 12 executives at Mysore Breweries that he could succeed – initially they laughed in his face. Backed by the managing director and brewmaster, experiments to replicate the elusive flavour in Karan's mind – 'refreshing and smooth' – were carried out and an initial brew sent to England. The brewery staff pledged their time and skill; Karan and his business partner at the time took full commercial risk. Shared commitment between the brewery and Cobra Beer helped to develop deep trust between them, which remains to this day.

In the early days of Cobra Beer, Karan and his business partner did not have time to think consciously about corporate governance. Survival was the main driver of action, yet there was an immediate recognition that survival depended on the support of customers and suppliers. Building trust was essential for survival and it had to be done right along the supply chain. Finance was a crucial issue and depended on building trust with shareholders and banks, as well as finding trade credit. Survival depended on Karan's key value of integrity – he insisted on never cutting corners. It took six major attempts to be sure that the product was exactly right for the market place.

Integrity helped to build trust but creativity and innovation were needed to keep the support of stakeholders. Problems were solved by ingenuity in order to maintain impetus. The business started with direct sales to Indian restaurants but could only expand by involving distributors. Lack of support was overcome by granting Gandhi Oriental Foods exclusivity within the M25 in exchange for a £100 000 credit facility to gear up the supply chain from India. Barclays guaranteed the funds and NatWest discounted the Bills of Exchange. This arrangement never failed and ensured product availability to support the growth of sales.

Having a clear vision and mission gave Karan the confidence to promote Cobra Beer relentlessly. His confidence helped to overcome resistance to 'yet another beer'. Once tried, because of consumer acceptance of the product, it was easy to obtain repeat orders. To make restaurateurs promote Cobra Beer the initial order had to be for a minimum of five cases (which Karan undertook to take back if an honest trial was unsuccessful). Having a minimum order size triggers commitment and opens the way to building loyalty.

Karan has gone out of his way to stay loyal to those who supported him in launching Cobra Beer. Among these was the manager of the warehouse who supported him even though his superiors were not enthusiastic. Over the years that relationship has developed with both supporting each other, sharing problems and working in total transparency. Cobra Beer still uses its original warehouse, though the volumes are now much more substantial.

The 'Indian' restaurant trade is dominated by Bangladeshis, who own two-thirds of restaurants. Of the rest, some half are Pakistani, other Nepalese, Sri Lankan and Indian owned. This has meant that Karan had to bring a degree of diplomacy into his relationships. Here again trust was essential in securing mutual benefit.

As Cobra Beer expanded it needed to focus on recruitment. From the beginning it had seen its staff as stakeholders in the business; they were selected to be self-reliant and multi-functional and trained to understand all aspects of the company and its relationships. People were recruited to grow with the business and share its success. Salaries are above average; when Cobra Beer is floated on the Stock Exchange, employees will have privileged access to shares.

An example of personal growth is the Sales Director, Samson Sohail. Cobra Beer started with two salesmen; in 1993 it recruited two more. Among the candidates was a young immigrant Pakistani, Samson, who had poor English but was desperate for a job. When he failed to be selected, he begged to be taken on, even if it meant being paid solely on a commission basis. He was given a month to hit a running rate of 100 cases per week. By week two he had hit the target, working all hours and committed to increase his productivity. Samson is now on Cobra's board of directors. At one stage he had been tempted to run his own business but loyalty to Cobra Beer prevailed.

Another director, Christopher Rendle, had been brought up in India and speaks fluent Hindi. He was very successful at Cobra but was poached by another company offering a major equity stake. He left with the blessing of Karan Bilimoria but returned within six months. He missed the passion at Cobra Beer and the culture of valuing people.

Although Karan ensures that there is a culture of trust and encouragement in Cobra Beer he is alert to the risk of 'bad apples'. Dishonesty is not tolerated and ill discipline is subject to a regime of warning and correction. There are no office politics at Cobra Beer, both because there is no idle time to encourage mischief and because communication with and between staff is totally open. Karan operates an 'open door' policy and is always available to staff.

When he started at Ernst & Young, Karan was encouraged by his father to see starting 'at the bottom' as an opportunity. He advised his son to do whatever he was asked willingly and to do even more. This 'extra mile' philosophy is part of the culture at Cobra Beer, which seeks to develop an efficient and happy team. Employees at Cobra Beer are subject to few rules – there are no office times, no dress code and no rules saying that drinking is not permitted. The culture ensures that rules are not needed and that employees behave sensibly. In the same way that Karan never asks for exclusivity from his customers (preferring that their clientele has a choice of beers) he does not seek to tie down his staff. The commitment they offer makes this unnecessary.

Sustainability is a key dimension of corporate governance. Karan Bilimoria believes that mobility and foresight are crucial to sustain success. Cobra Beer has a strategic plan up to 2010 and a three-year operating plan in detail. There is a set of personal objectives for each year which is shared by the whole team. This ensures that there are no silos or mixed agendas in the business. Karan sees the chief executive officer (CEO) as being an all-rounder, coaching and encouraging the team, who brings specialist skills to bear on specific issues. He admits that each is better than him as a specialist, even though he has sufficient knowledge of each specialism to interact with every team member. This multi-competence is encouraged in each of them through changing roles and collaboration on projects. Often team members spot issues missed by external advisers. It was the finance director who discovered the registration of 'Mogul' in the USA, not the trademark specialist. The search is now on for a suitable trademark to use in the company's expansion into North America.

In addition to five executive directors, Cobra Beer has two external directors. Karan was a member of Laura Tyson's 2003 taskforce to find new sources of independent directors in society. Cobra Beer is now an international company and needs a wide range of influences in its board deliberations. The staff resembles a miniature United Nations and board members include a Kenyan, two Britons, a Pakistani and an Indian. A Briton and American/Dutch are non-executive directors, and were known to Karan at Cambridge. He recognises that he does not yet meet all Higgs criteria, and has appointed a further non-executive director, a Kenyan. When Cobra Beer floats it is recognised that an independent chairman will be needed; at present Karan acts as chairman and CEO, though a non-executive director chairs the Annual General Meeting (AGM).

The AGM of Cobra Beer is a significant event. As many as 50 people may be present even though there are only 20 equity shareholders, since Karan Bilimoria owns 72 per cent of ordinary shares. All 80 preference shareholders are invited to participate (but not vote) and the company's various advisers are present. Following the meeting there is a reception and a meal at an Indian restaurant.

Even in its days of early struggle Cobra Beer used the best advisers to guide its divisions. Just before his marriage in 1993 Karan Bilimoria engaged Grant Thornton as financial advisers even though they were more expensive than many alternatives. When the government's Small Loan Guarantee scheme was launched, banks were offering £250 000 maximum investments; Grant Thornton pressed for a £1 000 000 company valuation and managed to find a 'business angel' to invest £50 000 to show confidence. The bank agreed to provide a £200 000 loan. At the time Cobra Beer had been exploring a venture capital option but Grant Thornton steered the company towards the government scheme. All advisers to Cobra Beer are expected to work closely with the company.

Cobra Beer is a entrepreneur-owned company and has a few family members among its employees. This is not an intended policy but family members may apply for vacancies and be judged openly on their merits. A first cousin of Karan left his job as finance director in a listed company at the time Cobra Beer was recruiting. Grant Thornton interviewed him, with others, and recommended him. Karan is conscious of the need to separate business and family issues if Cobra Beer is to be floated on the Stock Exchange. He is considering the 'family council' model, developed by Sir Adrian Cadbury, to enable family issues to be discussed outside the company and misunderstandings avoided.

Even though Cobra Beer started as a partnership of two people, Karan Bilimoria states that 50:50 arrangements rarely last. Every enterprise needs an undisputed leader if it is to avoid fragmenting under pressure. A key role of such a leader is to establish policies which bind the enterprise together and enable it to focus on survival and success.

In 20 years' time Cobra Beer should be a global brand, selling beer and other fruits of years of diversification. One fundamental challenge to Cobra Beer is to handle growth without weakening its entrepreneurial spirit. Karan Bilimoria has a mental model of growth through encouraging others to innovate. This would require effective systems and controls, but would be based on delegation and trust. It would need to avoid the idealism (and fate) of King Arthur's Round Table but be based on enlightened self-interest, encouraging freedom and flexibility and ensuring an equitable allocation of resources.

Karan Bilimoria is sensitive to potential threats and uses techniques, such as strengths, weaknesses, opportunities and threats (SWOT) analysis to monitor Cobra Beer's market positioning. He talks to competitors to understand their concerns. One issue which concerns Karan is the thirst for cash created by growth and the need to strengthen the balance sheet of Cobra Beer to cushion unexpected shocks.

The perspective of the company is also changing. As well as selling beer to accompany Indian meals, it now also focuses on a total experience. Beer may be consumed at any time and almost any place – Cobra Beer needs to be available to meet such demands. Cobra Beer was developed for sale in bottles; it is now available in more than 5000 Indian restaurants, in major supermarkets and off-licenses, and even at Lord's cricket ground. Consumers increasingly travel and want to find their favourite beer wherever they may be. Consumer expectations are heightened by a wealth of choice – consumer products need to focus on moving their quality ever upwards to meet these expectations.

Cobra Beer is deeply engaged in corporate social responsibility. It is involved with several charities, and sponsors sports and other events which enrich communities. Corporate social responsibility is not a fad or public relations exercise. It is a means of building relationships with communities, bringing benefits to those communities and strengthening the business of the company involved.

Karan Bilimoria has built in 13 years a business that has created and filled a niche in a growing market for Indian food and lifestyle. He has done this by focusing firmly on his mission of creating and selling a unique beer, and by looking constantly to the long term, rather than cutting corners. His success is due both to his entrepreneurial spirit but also to his ability to build lasting relationships with all stakeholders in his enterprise. He has steered his ship with a steady helm and his compass has been 'aspire and achieve against all odds'.

Diageo – is it possible to create a business with a soul?

In December 2003 Paul Walsh, Chief Executive of Diageo, spoke to an audience at the Institute of Business Ethics about his company and his mission to give a soul to a business in the sensitive sector of alcoholic drinks. With the merger of Grand Metropolitan and Guinness there had been a major rationalisation of both businesses, followed by the sale of non-drinks interests. As a result of their restructuring, and the absorption subsequently of the spirits division of Seagrams, Diageo had become the largest full range alcohol business in the world.

In order to give Diageo a soul, Paul Walsh needed to revolutionise its culture, create a new set of values to guide the company and develop matching behaviours at all levels of an organisation with nearly 25 000 employees and operating in 180 countries worldwide. Diageo had a number of successful drinks brands (with nine out of the top 20 worldwide) but it needed a single soul to achieve sustainable success.

What does Paul Walsh mean by 'soul'? In broad terms it comprises the intangible assets of a business, rather like 'body' equates to the tangible assets. To achieve a holistic performance a company must be outstanding at managing both tangible and intangible assets. Tangible assets are easier to value than intangible assets, but they are often consumed in running the business; intangible assets are usually difficult to quantify but easy to recognise, for example, as brands and reputation. Such assets need to be nurtured but are capable of generating substantial growth in business and of great longevity. Paul Walsh's approach to holistic business management is that of a supercharged 'balanced scorecard'.

Diageo approached the issue of developing a soul to match its successful and profitable body on two fronts. Firstly it was concerned to create a culture of compliance, even though its business is unregulated in most markets except the USA. Paul Walsh reasoned that to act as if within a regulatory regime was to reduce the potential threat of regulation. He appointed a Global Compliance Director, Peter Cowap, who has operated in the highly regulated banking industry, with a remit to construct an appropriately similar process within Diageo worldwide and at all levels. The actual culture is one which seeks to foster integrity rather than just compliance. Peter Cowap reports to the General Counsel, Tim Proctor, who sits on the Executive Committee. He also reports to the Audit and Risk Committee which is chaired by Paul Walsh. He is in frequent contact with the Group Chief Executive, because of the need to deal with regulatory developments and the issues emerging from the Sarbanes-Oxley Act in the USA and their worldwide repercussions.

The second front is cultural. Diageo needs to sustain and develop its successful business by developing a soul to match its body. In the same way that brand values have been developed by global consistency of quality, those brand values need to be sustained by quality behaviours. The interaction of both qualities creates a self-reinforcing process which drives further growth. Paul Walsh set out to transform Diageo and make it more holistic. He has created a 'strategic architecture' to bind all stakeholders into the development of the company. Stakeholders include media, non-government organizations (NGOs) and others excluded by most companies because a holistic process includes critics as well as partners. Having seen the development of class actions in the USA, Diageo needs to learn from the problems of the tobacco and food industries. Unlike those and other problem industries (for example, chemicals), alcohol has many supporters, not least in the medical profession. Nevertheless Diageo is aware of the need to disarm potential critics through demonstrably responsible behaviour. To do so it supports standards bodies like the Portman Group and sponsors programmes such as bartender training, which help to restrain binge drinking and other excesses.

Internally Diageo has established structures and processes to help generate quality behaviours. Employees are guided by a number of codes, the most important being the 'Code of Business Conduct' into which the others are subsumed. The code covers responsibilities, problem solving, obligations to consumers, citizenship, the public arena (political, religious, charities, and so on), sales and commercial transactions, shareholder obligations, personal integrity, protecting competitive assets (for example, brands), and agency relationships. Each employee accepts a written obligation to observe the code in its entirety; this written obligation becomes part of the contract of employment. All senior managers are required annually to complete a certificate of compliance, having conferred in detail with their direct reports. All employees worldwide have access to a 'Speak Up Helpline' to enable them to report issues of concern where their normal reporting channel is inappropriate or unresponsive. 'Helpline' calls go directly to Peter Cowap, the company secretary or the security director. The legal and HR departments are not involved at the reporting stage.

Diageo has established a number of values which act as beacons for guiding daily conduct. These are:

- Proud of what we do (world leaders set themselves challenging standards)
- Being the best (sustaining excellent performance)
- Passionate about consumers (building long-term relationships)
- Freedom to succeed (investing in sound business practices).

Unlike many companies Diageo limits its values to four. The effectiveness of value sets depends on their ability to shape behaviours; this requires that people can remember them and that they are relevant to the business. Diageo scores well on both counts.

The fourth of Diageo's values is 'freedom to succeed' and Diageo uses this to drive the achievement of the first three. Few other companies have such a commitment to empowering their employees and this is probably the main strategy for embedding the behaviours needed to deliver Paul Walsh's aim of 'operating in world-leading ways'. According to Gareth Williams, Diageo's HR Director, 'releasing the potential of our people' is one of the company's core strategic imperatives. Development in Diageo is focused on 'people' and 'brands'. A two-day high-performance coaching programme spearheads the drive to release potential in Diageo's nearly 25 000 staff. To date some 4000 employees have undergone this programme and are seeding interest in improvement among their colleagues.

Mentoring is also being encouraged at all levels, initially through regular development conversations between managers and individual employees. These initiatives drive the specific development and training activities which build the 'freedom to succeed' of each employee. Development in each of Diageo's main market areas is supplemented by a programme of trans-national secondments which at 300 represents 10 per cent of all managers and will be increased by at least 10 per cent over the next four years. Recruitment is now open to all globally which should enrich the ethnic mix in all of Diageo's operating centres. All employees are encouraged to be active in their local community and to balance their work commitments with a fulfilling home life. In order to channel employees' released potential into the business, Diageo has a collection of brand-building programmes which inculcate best practice from all sources and help to achieve the values of being the best and of having pride in what the company does.

It is intended to add a fifth value – 'Value each other'. This should help to lubricate internal processes and hopefully to embed the value set in the company psyche. Diageo has been doing an annual survey for some five years to gauge the response of employees to the values. Results to date are disappointing, since deeds do not yet match the values. Nevertheless the response rate is improving and there is greater recognition of the need to 'live the values'. The annual compliance process has been more successful, since it is structured and closely monitored. Increasing public interest in issues such as child labour, sweat shops and corruption has given a cutting edge to compliance reporting, and in Diageo reporting goes to the top of the business.

Diageo has a board structure which has a preponderance of non-executive directors; eight out of ten board members are non-executive and are actively involved in the work of the audit, nomination and remuneration committees. Paul Walsh chairs the executive committee, which links the board with corporate management, and the citizenship and brand committees. Non-executive directors are involved in these last two committees because of their strategic importance. The compliance reporting is monitored by the Audit Committee which brings significant issues to the attention of the board.

Diageo sees itself as a 'fun business'. Its chosen role is to encourage social intercourse, to enable consumers to enjoy themselves and to help the wheels of society to turn easily. Its staff are selected to be sociable and to help consumers to lead enjoyable and fulfilling lives. The company is aware of the 'dark side' of alcohol, solitary addicted drinking and uncontrollable changes of mood induced by excessive consumption. Diageo helped to create the Portman Group and has developed a 'marketing code' within the Code of Business Conduct which sets clear guidelines for marketing alcoholic drinks, subject to local law and customs.

The Code of Marketing Practice for Alcohol Beverages establishes clear and detailed 'dos and don'ts' for key areas of business promotion. It covers compliance with laws and regulations, underage drinking prevention, responsible drinking provisions, respect for abstinence, preventing offensive advertising, not promoting alcohol content, evaluating medicinal or therapeutic value of alcohol, drinking and driving, not promoting social or sexual success through alcohol, avoiding anti-social activities, and promoting responsible drinking. Compliance with the code is mandatory for all employees or agents of Diageo and it is supported by a programme of education for those who serve and those who drink alcohol. Diageo takes great care to attune its advertising and promotional messages to the code and to local sensitivities in different markets. Issues such as the misselling of 'alcopops' to children present constant difficulties and the code needs constant enforcement to prevent malpractice.

Now that the Code of Business Conduct is in place, it is being enforced with rigour. The first principle is that top management has to 'live the code' and be seen to be doing so and seeking to achieve ever higher standards. The re-organisation following the merger offered the opportunity to pick a top team committed to higher standards. The compliance programme helps to ensure that these are maintained since managers put their job on the line in reporting compliance in detail. Since the programme started, some people have been disciplined and a few dismissed for non-observance. The 'Speak Up Helpline' averages two calls per month and has triggered sanctions in a growing number of cases. Initially there was some resistance from the marketing area to the 'marketing code' as it was seen as a threat to business development. Much of this has now been defused by staff transfers and a sustained programme of training. Paul Walsh has personally worked for compliance in the marketing area with growing success. Problems have also been met with advertising agencies, for example a Smirnoff Ice advertisement in London Underground seemed to mock the Taiwanese and caused parliamentary questions in Taipei, but agencies now understand that Diageo is different from some others in the drinks industry. Marketing was more 'laddish' in its attitudes in the past; the growing number of women in senior positions is curbing many excesses. Progress is also underpinned by the beginning of a shift from compliance to values-based behaviours.

Paul Walsh is looking to develop an iconic brand like Coca-Cola. At present Diageo has dozens of brands, several iconic in their own right (like Johnnie Walker) and its umbrella brand, like that of Unilever, is under-developed. Will Diageo follow Nestlé in creating a single integrating brand? To do so would be a logical next step after the disposal of non-drinks businesses and would integrate a group where loyalties have not always been to the centre. Diageo is favoured in having products with high gross margins, averaging some 25 per cent, compared with beer and wine with some 10 per cent. To grow its business in the premium drinks sector, Diageo has to capture and consolidate the high ground, both in market share and in brand loyalty. Paul Walsh sees 'soul' as the spiritual link between Diageo and its worldwide clientele of all ages. Good citizenship is essential to sustain this link and the Code of Business Conduct is the means of delivering success on a sustainable basis. The code is in place and its effectiveness will be judged both by its ability to bring the behaviour of individual employees, and key groups of employees, consistently in line with the five values, and by the verdict of external stakeholders on its validity for them.

Scottish and Southern Energy

Dr Bruce Farmer has been Chairman of Scottish and Southern Energy plc for nearly four years. The company was formed through a merger of Scottish Hydro plc and Southern Electric plc in December 1998 and has acquired other businesses, for example, SWALEC since that date. Scottish and Southern is ranked 41st in the FTSE 100 index and is a major energy group on an European scale.

Bruce Farmer believes that successful companies are built with patience and care over time. Many utilities rushed to diversify away from their regulated base when privatised and most have regretted doing so. Severn Trent's success with Biffa has been an exception but was deemed to be expensive at the time and has taken time to fructify. Scottish and Southern has anchored itself in the energy sector (even avoiding the acquisition of water companies) and has paid fair prices for its acquisitions in the electricity and gas sectors. It refused to overpay for MEB and SEEBORD and has focused on organic growth primarily. Scottish and Southern has a strong operational focus, aiming to achieve excellence in operating efficiency and customer satisfaction. It has won national awards for many years in both dimensions, including the JD Power accolade for customer satisfaction.

Corporate governance in Scottish and Southern is businesslike. It focuses on meeting all the Hampel and Higgs criteria and on having a workman-like relationship with its regulators, Ofgen and FSA. The company also encourages activities to protect the environment, not least in protecting woodland sites where it operates. Its policies were commended in an Early Day Motion in Parliament in March 2004, and it has twice won 'Best in Sector' awards in the Business in the Environment Index of Corporate Environmental Engagement. The company sees external corporate responsibility as an integral part of its work to build a successful business.

Bruce Farmer sees the building of a strong board as the key driver of effective governance. The board provides leadership to the whole company, determines its strategic direction and shapes its culture. He sees his role as the architect of the board and as clerk of works in building and sustaining it. The separation of the roles of chairman and chief executive is fundamental to the achievement of the balance of power and the trade-off between the short- and long-term performance of the company which enables it to achieve excellence. Bruce believes that the chairman has to set the tone of the company both internally and externally so that it stands out from its peers. A winning company with a reputation for integrity wins and retains the support of all stakeholders and builds long-term shareholder value.

Bruce Farmer believes in a board with sufficient members to provide a range of expertise and experience to create challenging debates and explore issues from many angles. Some ten to twelve members typically provide this richness of input and the dynamic needed to produce well-reasoned and tested decisions. He believes that the Higgs balanced board, with a small majority of independent directors, is the best model. As chairman he is alert to the need to avoid capture of the board by executive directors (who have deeper knowledge of the company's operations) but is concerned to develop his non-executive (independent) directors to provide a challenging debate.

Great care is taken in selecting directors. Bruce chairs the nomination committee because of the need for a rigorous process of selection. All appointments are made through the use of head-hunters – this ensures that candidates seen by the nomination committee are 'pre-qualified' and avoids any suspicion of advancing the cause of candidates known to any of the directors. All shortlisted candidates are interviewed in depth and have psychometric assessment. Short-listed candidates are seen by all members of the board so that the final selection is made by them all. Great care is taken to balance the skills and experience of the board. Bruce found himself recently with too many accountants on the board, so his next appointment was Kevin Smith of GKN – an engineer. This appointment also provides support for the chief operating officer (COO) in day-to-day management.

Bruce Farmer believes in actively developing the ability of new directors to contribute to the work of the board. All have a personal induction in which he is involved. This includes visits to key sites and sitting in on management meetings. New directors may select external courses to meet their needs; this facility continues during their tenure of office.

All directors are subject to an annual peer review. This is a rigorous one-to-one personal interview and focuses on their contribution to the board and the company over the last year. Bruce Farmer believes that all directors have a 'sell by' date and this review reveals any symptoms of complacency or tiredness. Most non-executive directors serve two three-year terms; a longer tenure is unusual. Having lost a CEO at Morgan Crucible to illness, Bruce is sensitive to the need for succession and contingency planning. The board is involved in this process so that being 'hit by a bus' is accounted for in all appointments.

Scottish and Southern Energy has a board of eleven directors, six of whom are independent (including a part-time chairman). The board has six committees:

- Audit Committee (chaired by René Médori) – independent
- Remuneration Committee (chaired by David Payne) – independent
- Nomination Committee (chaired by Dr Bruce Farmer) – independent chairman
- Risk Committee (chaired by Colin Hood, the COO)
- Executive Committee (chaired by Ian Marchant, the CEO)
- Safety and Environmental Advisory Committee.

The Risk Committee oversees the Group's trading activities, which are regulated by the Financial Services Authority (FSA). It also monitors the board's responsibilities under the Turnbull Report. The Safety and Environmental Advisory Committee provides support to the Group staff responsible for health and safety and for environmental protection. These are issues in which the board takes a close interest.

Bruce Farmer is keen that the board should follow in detail the FSA Listing Rules and the corporate governance codes which they specify. He has moved to ensure that the requirements of the Higgs Report are met by the Group, principally by appointing three 'independent directors' (as defined by Higgs) – Sir Robert Smith, René Médori and Susan Rice. The deputy chairman, Sir Robert Smith, is the senior independent director as defined by Higgs. The board is concerned to restrain the use of the external auditor for non-audit services and has a formal policy for controlling the use of external advisors.

The work of the board is governed by five key ethical principles:

- Seeking to meet the needs of, and contributing to the welfare of, customers by supplying energy to them and the communities that the board serves, in a way which is reliable, safe and represents value for money.
- Achieving the highest standards of health and safety performance so that employees and contractors are able to carry out their responsibilities in the safest possible manner, reflecting the fact that safety will never be compromised for business interests or operational pressures.
- Being actively responsible towards current and future generations by prioritising and continually improving the environmental performance of its activities.
- Enabling employees to derive the maximum possible benefit from their employment with the Group, through participation in its affairs, active encouragement of share ownership and the maintenance of effective policies on issues such as equal opportunities.
- Taking proper account of the interests of the communities in which Scottish and Southern Energy operates and assisting in projects which fall within agreed criteria, including the interests of young people, health and safety environment and energy efficiency.

The Group actively encourages best practice on the part of contractors and suppliers through the evaluation of their policies and approaches to health, safety and environment issues. Their practices have to equal the Group's standards or they will not be employed.

Scottish and Southern Energy has a 'whistle-blowing' procedure which enables employees to alert the company to activities likely to cause it damage. This involves a 'hot line' to the Audit Committee chairman who can evaluate any call and take appropriate action. This line has not yet been used in earnest.

Bruce Farmer sees the role of a chairman as both the leader of the board and as a roving ambassador. Externally he is active in meeting shareholders and in keeping the Group's name to the fore in the City and in industry forums. Internally he spends at least one day each month visiting Group sites and holding 'no holds barred' question and answer sessions. He makes a point of being visible to staff and approachable without compromising the authority of executive management. Knowing that the Group is run openly and effectively builds confidence among staff and key external stakeholders. The board avoids 'fat-cattery' for itself and has increased its dividend by 30 per cent in real terms since 1999 when Group results were first reported. It has also delivered a consistent increase in shareholder value since the merger both through trading and by judicious purchase and cancellation of company shares. The balance sheet of Scottish and Southern Energy is one of the strongest in the global utility sector. Bruce Farmer has been very successful in building a strong board to grow a world-class company.

BP Amoco – a return to basics?

This case study was written in the aftermath of the major mergers in the late 1990s which took BP to a leading position as a global company. It highlights the steps needed to integrate businesses with a British and an American approach to corporate governance which differ in board structure and reporting patterns. Since this study was written BP has evolved further towards a British model of board (with five executive and twelve non-executive directors) without major difficulty.

INTRODUCTION

The development of joint stock companies, and subsequent legislation to limit investor liability, were driven by the need to attract and retain capital. The governance of joint stock companies was delegated to a board of directors who were responsible for organising the business and directing it in the interests of shareholders. Directors, unlike shareholders, were not protected by limited liability, in order to ensure that their stewardship remained sharp and focused on shareholder interests.

As companies grew and their operations became more complex the board found increasing difficulty in exercising effective oversight. Key managers were required to report to the board and, in time, some were invited to join the board in order to provide an effective link between the business and the representatives of its owners. In much of Europe a two-tier board structure developed, with the Supervisory Board representing owners (and later banks and trades unions) and an Executive Board managing the company. US boards typically comprised a majority of non-executive directors, leading to a situation where effective power was often exercised outside the boardroom. It is interesting to note that Peter Drucker never mentions the board as a factor in the management process!

British boards gradually evolved to the point where most had a majority of executive directors. Some British boards do not have non-executive directors; their involvement is stronger in larger company boards, but totally missing in many smaller companies.

Traditionally British non-executive directors have come from the ranks of 'the great and the good', bringing titles and connections but dividing their time among a variety of different board appointments. Over time this allowed power to move into the hands of executive directors, making it difficult for the whole board to understand the full implications of many of the decisions which they endorsed. The failure of Rolls Royce and the decline of Midland Bank are two sober examples of the consequences of this development. The demise of British and Commonwealth and Coloroll are two of the many scandals which helped to force the issue of corporate governance onto the agenda of the City of London, beginning a process which culminated in the Cadbury, Greenbury and Hampel Codes.

THE CRISIS

While economies are strong and wealth continues to expand, the inadequacies of governance are a secondary issue. In the nineteenth century, company failures were frequent but lack of knowledge made it easier to escape from accountability. Investment in South American railways was a high risk, high return activity; lack of detail about the operations in which investors placed their money was not seen as unusual. It was expected to be risky and information was best kept secret in order to win a competitive advantage; those who wanted a safe investment could buy Consols!

The blame for the 1929 Crash and subsequent failures was laid on the major governments rather than on business. With the New Deal and the preparations for war, confidence returned progressively; after the war a boom buried memories of the Crash for many investors. In the USA the growing sense of world leadership built confidence in American business which was only challenged when Japanese industry won the high ground in a number of key product sectors. In the UK nationalisation and poor management led to a progressive loss of relative position in world markets and a focus on short-term returns. On the continent of Europe there was greater industrial harmony due to policies which involved labour and business in a 'social contract', under which employment was protected and union pressures were moderated. This delayed the impact of competitive forces and the consequent challenge to their model of corporate governance.

The crisis which raised the profile of corporate governance began in the USA with the growth of world competition and the relative failure of several major US businesses, including Ford, General Motors and International Business Machines (IBM). The Crash of 1987 severely jolted confidence in business investment. Institutional investors had expected growing returns since the 1960s; when competition started to bite, companies had indulged in take-overs in order to grow profits rapidly but the quality of their earnings was not sustainable. Investors initially reacted by churning their portfolio but this added cost and achieved little. Gradually investors began to take a more active interest in key stockholdings, led by role models such as Berkshire Hathaway in the USA. In the UK institutional investors, such as Hermes, have become less tolerant of poor performance as they are increasingly rated against each other and called to account for uncompetitive results by their own investors.

THE NEW ACCOUNTABILITY

The Organization for Economic Co-operation and Development (OECD) Report on Corporate Governance (April 1998) states: 'The board of directors – or in some nations, the board of auditors – is uniquely positioned as the internal corporate mechanism for holding management accountable to stockholders' (Chapter 1 Section 27). In his article 'The Professional Board' (*The Business Lawyer*, November 1995) Ira M. Millstein lays out the foundations for a board which will be both more accountable and more professional. By 'professional' he infers that directors will be more effective and not just members of an elite whose sole function is to sit on as many boards as possible. Mr Millstein sees a growing 'activation' of company boards in the USA in response to failures in company performance, pressure from institutional shareholders, the effects of emerging globalisation and a demand for higher standards of governance. Boards are to become proactive and independent rather than reacting to events and endorsing management decisions without debate.

The board is, therefore, accountable primarily to shareholders but increasingly faces demands for recognition from other constituencies, including customers, staff, suppliers and government. In the UK this case for wider accountability has been developed by 'Tomorrow's Company' to cover a broad range of stakeholders across the community whose support is needed to have 'a licence to operate'. Companies are now 'accountable' to Greenpeace and in Italy to the Mafia – how many masters will the board be required to serve? BP resists this 'slippery slope' and sees itself, as a private sector company, accountable solely to shareholders. It is, of course, very sensitive to the impact of its operations on the wider community.

A NEW (OLD) MODEL

A report by Professor Eddy Wymeersch of the University of Ghent, 'Corporate Governance in Western Europe: Structures and Comparisons' (European Bank for Reconstruction and Development [EBRD] 'Law in Transition', Autumn 1999) reveals a very concentrated pattern of share ownership in most of Continental Europe and a contrasting dispersal of ownership in the UK. He deduces that control lies primarily with banks and major investors in Continental Europe while British managers have been able to dominate many British boards and exercise power with limited constraint. Boards in the USA are also less constrained and it may be that the Anglo-Saxon penchant for aggressive mergers and violent cost cutting has been a result of under restrained executive ambition. Recent evidence indicates that Continental Europe may be beginning to follow the Anglo-Saxon example, for example, BNP's contested take-over of Paribas.

An excellent example of a 'friendly' merger is that of British Petroleum (BP) and Amoco. This created the fifteenth largest company in the world, operating on a global scale and with shareholders in many countries. The merger was completed in December 1998 and 60 per cent of shareholders had held shares in BP and 40 per cent of Amoco shares. BP is quoted on the London Stock Exchange but, because of the weight of its business in the USA, reports in US dollars. Since the merger Atlantic Richfield (Arco) and Burmah Castrol have been taken over by BP. The acquisition of Arco initially produced a preponderance of US shareholders, but they now hold less than 33 per cent of BP shares.

The board of BP is currently an amalgamation of the previous boards of BP and Amoco. It has 17 members of whom 12 are non-executive directors. The chairman is Peter Sutherland, having earlier been co-chairman with Larry Fuller, and the deputy chairman is Sir Ian Prosser. Larry Fuller was, until his retirement in April 2000, an executive director in order to support the process of merging (having been chairman and chief executive of Amoco). The chief executive is Lord Browne and deputy chief executive, Rodney Chase.

Apart from some temporary compromises and difficulties in integrating reward packages, the board of BP Amoco seems to follow a typically British model. In fact it is based on a model adapted from the thinking of John Carver, the American voluntary sector governance guru, which imposes a clearer separation of powers between the board and executive management than has been evident in British companies for many years. Carver believes that his model, 'with only slight alteration, is completely applicable to business corporations'. This implies that a board should:

- understand the shareholders' view of the purpose of the company
- account to shareholders for performance in achieving that purpose
- find, direct, monitor and remunerate the chief executive.

PURPOSE

In the board governance policies of BP Amoco it is stated that 'the purpose of BP Amoco is business and to maximise long-term shareholder value by selling goods and services'. This statement clarifies the long-term focus of the company and mandates the board to resist pressures from the City or key employees to maximise short-term results. Relationships with stakeholders may only be developed in accordance with powers delegated by shareholders to the board.

ACCOUNTING FOR PERFORMANCE

Accounting for performance to shareholders is a challenge for a company which has over half a million members of whom 93 per cent are individuals. Legally all shareholders must be treated equally but many are inactive and some 90 per cent of the share capital is held by members each owning over 100 000 shares. The traditional means of reporting to members, through annual and half yearly reports and at general meetings, are increasingly inadequate. BP Amoco issues a number of supplementary reports which are available to shareholders, and it runs an active Internet website. Large institutional shareholders have meetings with directors in order to minimise the risk of surprises and maintain confidence in the direction of the company's affairs. Echoes of these briefings can usually be found in the financial press by smaller shareholders who actively manage their share portfolios. For all quoted companies voting remains a contentious issue for small shareholders as the proxy votes of major shareholders are usually pledged in support of proposals from the board which may be controversial, for example, share buyback or share dividends. Small shareholders could use an intermediary to amalgamate their votes but this has not happened on any significant scale. Because of the wide dispersal of its shareholders BP now requires a poll for all substantive motions which gives due weighting to proxy votes; only procedural matters are voted on by a show of hands of those present at the meeting.

CHIEF EXECUTIVE

BP Amoco follows the Cadbury recommendation to separate the roles of chairperson and chief executive. This practice is less common in the USA where the senior employee is often the president or chief operating officer. BP Amoco's adaptation of John Carver's model has three distinct elements – shareholders, the board and the CEO. The chief executive is the most senior employee and the bridge between the board and management. The chief executive is accountable to the whole board (and not individual directors) for the activities of the management team. The board may deal with other employees only through the chief executive.

The board is required to find, direct, monitor and remunerate the chief executive and, if necessary, to dismiss him or her. As the chief executive controls all resources in the company, great skill is needed in managing the interface between him or her and the board. At BP Amoco there is a clear contract between the board and the chief executive which specifies the corporate purpose (goals) and the measures by which performance in meeting it will be judged. John Carver defines this as the board–executive relationship, which encompasses the ends (corporate purpose) and executive limitations policies. BP Amoco also has an executive limitations policy which defines boundaries to the freedom of the chief executive in choosing means to achieve goals. The details of the policy are confidential but its scope may be summarised thus: 'The CEO will not cause or permit any practice, activity or decision that is in violation of commonly accepted business practice or professional ethics or in excess of the limits of authority granted by the board to the CEO.' The policy naturally covers health, safety, the environment, financial distress, internal control, risk, treatment of employees and political issues. The chief executive has considerable discretion and may exceed it, if he or she deems it necessary to do so. Should they do so they will be called to account for their action.

All reporting is related to the goals and to the corporate plans and budgets which reflect short- and medium-term progress towards those goals. The board does not focus on the activities of the chief executive, which are purely incidental to the activities within the total company, for which he or she is accountable.

BOARD COMMITTEES

The board of BP Amoco is supported by a small number of working committees whose role is as follows:

- *Chairman's Committee* (chairman and all non-executive directors)
  Develops policy on organisation and succession planning and performance assessment of the CEO.

- *Audit Committee* (six non-executive directors)
  Monitors all reporting, accounting, control and financial aspects of the company's activities, including the requirements of the Turnbull Report.

- *Ethics and Environment Assurance Committee* (six non-executive directors)
  Monitors all other non-financial aspects of the company's activities.

- *Remuneration Committee* (six non-executive directors)
  Develops policies for performance contracts and targets, and the relevant rewards for the chief executive and other executive directors.

- *Nomination Committee* (non-executive co-chairman, chief executive, any three non-executive directors)
  Assists the process of finding and appointing new directors.

All principal board committees are comprised of non-executive directors and great care is taken to ensure that they are able to exercise independent judgement. They must have no outside relationship with any members of executive management that could lead to accusations of conflict of interest or duty. Non-executive directors do not have service contracts, must offer themselves for re-election every third year and may be in office for a maximum of ten years.

COMPANY SECRETARY'S OFFICE

Unlike the situation in most other companies the role of the board of BP Amoco is distinct from the role of management of the business. This requires the company secretary's office to stand outside executive management structure, so that the company secretary reports solely and directly to the chairperson. Because of the complexity of the relationships of a global company like BP Amoco it has been decided that the board will focus on shareholder relationships; other relationships, for example, with customers and employees, are delegated to the chief executive. The board remains accountable to shareholders, of course, for the way these other relationships are handled and the company secretary's office processes shareholder queries and requests for information arising from this accountability.

The secretary of BP Amoco manages a small team which is focused exclusively on servicing the board and the needs of shareholders. This is a more specialised set of tasks than that of the normal company secretary. One function within the office is to keep abreast of the best thinking on corporate governance and board process, which is led by the Vice-President, Corporate Governance, Rodney Insall. This senior appointment, together with British Telecom's appointment of a director of corporate governance, may be the beginning of a trend to demonstrate commitment to corporate governance at the highest level in major companies. The BP Amoco company secretary's office resembles that of the French *secrétaire général* rather than the English model, due both to its particular role and the content of its workload. To discharge its own functions it requires the co-operation of relevant teams such as Public Affairs, Investor Relations and Equity Operations (Share Registrar). Where the board has retained authority over an issue, the company secretary's office must protect this authority and ensure that its use conforms to the board-executive relationship policy.

ISSUES OF GOVERNANCE FACING BP AMOCO

BP Amoco has needed to face the issue of integrating two different approaches to corporate governance. The board of BP had adopted in 1997 a set of governance policies which formed the basis for the policies detailed in this chapter. The Amoco board comprised 11 non-executive and two executive directors, and members of management attended board meetings as required. The board was led by a chairman and chief executive (Larry Fuller) but board committees comprised non-executive directors almost exclusively. There was an executive committee of the board which functioned between board meetings, as needed. Amoco non-executive directors believe that the new board has too many executive directors.

A major difficulty lay in reconciling reward packages. Not only were Amoco salaries higher than those for BP directors but Amoco had a share option scheme which had no performance conditions and was at a higher level than those achievable under the BP long-term performance plan. These difficulties were solved by establishing higher levels of reward which were conditional on meeting challenging targets.

An emerging issue for BP Amoco, following the merger with Arco, will be the preponderance of US investors and its enlarged American business base. There is already pressure for shareholder meetings to be held in the USA; this may be followed by pressure to be quoted on the New York Stock Exchange (avoiding the use of clumsy Accounting Deposit Receipts [ADRs]). Domicile will be a growing issue for all global companies and BP Amoco will not be exempt.

BP Amoco is facing a growing complexity in its relationships as its business becomes totally global. It is actively developing working links with stakeholders in all countries where it operates, seeking to be a good citizen as well as a provider of wealth. Like most major multinational companies, it is becoming a target of NGOs, many of which use shareholdings to push their own agenda, for example the environment of Alaska. This challenge is likely to worsen until NGOs are accountable to the societies which they seek to protect.

Another difficulty for the board is the development of strategy. This is the responsibility of the chief executive who regularly briefs the board on progress and uses away days to involve them in fuller detail. Since the board's primary role is seen as to act as the link between shareholders and the managers of the company and to oversee effective performance in achieving the corporate purpose, there is some hesitation in moving beyond the definition of goals to the determination of means of achieving them. The board prefers to act as a referee in terms of strategy rather than as a player, although it may sometimes find itself in the role of coach!

A very significant difficulty is the reluctance of institutional shareholders to meet non-executive directors. They want hard information and see access to the chief executive as the proper source for it. In the UK non-executive directors are seen as accessories, not real players. Investors find that their replies to questions frequently lack focus and content; when pressed about major decisions some non-executive directors may be inclined to blame professional advisers.

IMPLICATIONS FOR THE FUTURE ROLE OF THE BOARD

The board of BP Amoco has evolved to meet the challenge of ensuring accountability to shareholders. After a period in the UK in which the power of executive 'baronies' held too much sway in deciding the fate of companies, leading to ill-considered ventures and unstable structures which destroyed shareholder value, we may now have re-empowered the British company shareholder and have begun to revive the concept of stewardship in managing companies. Now that the saturnalia is over, how will boards develop into the future?

In the wider corporate world there seems to be a firm trend to dismantle the interlocking shareholdings which have characterised capitalism in Japan, Germany and other non-Anglo-Saxon markets. Shareholders will be freer to invest for value in a changing world but less able to manipulate policy in the companies in which they invest. We shall probably see greater openness in share ownership, even an erosion of the use of bearer shares in due course. The trading of shares should become more open and insider dealing and share manipulation harder to achieve. A more fluid market for shares as large cross-holdings are liquidated will make it easier to trade shares; this will return the initiative to shareholders and make company management more sensitive to its share rating. Where shares are held to match a stockmarket index, shareholders will need to manage their portfolio aggressively and be more demanding of competitive performance by management.

Most UK companies operate their board as an integrated team (at least towards the outside world!) so that presentations to institutional shareholders involve executive directors. BP Amoco follows this practice as institutional shareholders are reluctant to have relationships with non-executive directors (even with a part-time chairperson). The Hampel Code sees the board as an unit and focuses on its balance: 'The board should include a balance of executive and non-executive directors (including independent non-executives) such that no individual or small group of individuals can dominate the board's decision taking' (Code A3). In a British board with a majority of executive directors and a separate chairperson and chief executive it is difficult to act like an American board with a majority of non-executive directors and a combined chairperson and chief executive. While all directors share equally the responsibility for the success of the company, it will become increasingly difficult to maintain collegiate structures in the face of pressure from the media and analysts for 'star' contacts. How much may 'star' status have contributed to the erratic judgement and downfall of Bob Ayling of British Airways?

The board will also need to plan and manage the relationship of the company with outside constituencies or stakeholders, and with its own employees. These relationships are becoming more complex and many are involuntary, for example with NGOs. Failure to manage such relationships has damaged companies such as Shell and Exxon. Shareholders will need to be properly briefed on the issues and risks involved in identifying and managing such relationships. Failure to do so can bring devastating consequences, as in the case of Microsoft.

Globalisation will bring increasing pressure to perform on both institutional shareholders and the companies in which they invest. In the past, the media has tended to lionise individual business leaders, such as Asil Nadir of Polly Peck, often encouraging hubris and the destruction of shareholder value. In a more complex and dangerous world, leadership needs to be bolder yet more circumspect. The 'hero as leader' may motivate in the short term, but the long term is built by multiple talents and a sustained process of self-renewal. Capitalism began with the amateur board responsible solely to shareholders; it may need to develop the professional board, accountable to shareholders but answerable to a more complex and demanding world society.

6 Entrepreneurs and Family Companies

These case studies explore the phenomena of entrepreneurial business and of the related family business sector. The largest number of companies in any country fall into these categories and the dynamism of the best drives the economy. One trend which is not healthy is the progressive decline in family businesses, due both to weakening intrafamily loyalty and pressure for acquisitions by large groups. Fortunately there seems little decline in the birth-rate of new businesses; their independent existence may, however, be shortening due to insatiable mergers and acquisitions (M and A) activity.

Governance for entrepreneurs

The idea that entrepreneurs would have any time for corporate governance is counter-intuitive. It seems rather like mixing oil and water – an exercise in frustration and futility. In practice it may be more like making mayonnaise; achieving a delicate and unstable mixture which has unusual attractiveness.

Entrepreneurs do not all behave like pirates. The *Oxford English Dictionary* defines an entrepreneur as 'a person in effective control of a commercial undertaking'. This definition could apply to a manager as much as to a director; the essence of entrepreneurship is the undertaking of risk to achieve greater reward. The image of an entrepreneur as a pirate derives from the American 'trusts' of the nineteenth century and from modern serial entrepreneurs such as Richard Branson and Stelios Haji-Ioannou. In his article in the *Financial Times*, 'Understanding Entrepreneurship' (12 November 2003), Jonathan Guthrie sees different models of entrepreneur:

> *There are entrepreneurs who run their businesses in the structured way in which they all oversaw divisions of large companies. There are entrepreneurs who are entirely wrapped up in improving their offer to customers, leaving the boring wheeler-dealing to the paid help. There are shy entrepreneurs, who retreat from media overtures as assiduously as some extroverted entrepreneurs pursue them.*

Apart from an appetite for taking risk, the other main characteristic of entrepreneurs is a desire to control the destiny of their business. It is for this reason that many entrepreneurs shun the Stock Exchange and prefer to operate through private companies or networks of holdings which avoid constraint on their activities, for example Bentley Brothers. How can entrepreneurs come to terms with the 'stakeholder' economy which global interdependence and intrusive media have fostered?

RELATIONSHIPS

It is manifestly impossible to conduct business without having relationships. Even a sole trader needs customers and other relationships develop as a business becomes larger and more complex, requiring staff, suppliers, advisers, and so on. Some businesspeople operate by 'dividing and ruling' so that stakeholders are less likely to come together to challenge them. Robert Maxwell was skilful at manipulation and obfuscation so that he was never effectively accountable to anybody, though nobody trusted him. Without a basic level of trust, relationships are unstable and unproductive.

Trust is usually developed over time through using certain principles in personal and business relationships. These might be Lord Nolan's 'Principles of Public Life' – selflessness, integrity, objectivity, accountability, openness, honesty and leadership. 'Selflessness' is perhaps more appropriate to public life than to building business, yet a willingness to temper selfishness is essential in any relationship. Integrity, objectivity, accountability, openness and honesty are the basic building blocks of trust and are at the core of corporate governance. Leadership is the factor which gives purpose to these principles so that results can be achieved. For an entrepreneur the 'self' is the well-spring of all his or her actions; entrepreneurs often seem to need to prove themselves to justify their existence – *j'entreprends donc je suis!* Their 'id' is focused on achievement; it is the nature of that achievement which requires external governance.

Few entrepreneurs operate without significant external constraints. Those who try to do so usually find their activities restricted. The Russian oligarchs are now tethered by political constraints, much as the American trusts were dismantled a century earlier. Society needs entrepreneurs to build businesses to create the wealth needed for prosperity, yet it cannot allow them to operate outside the rules which sustain it. Governance is a key dimension of those rules.

FINANCE

One major constraint on most entrepreneurs is finance. A few, such as Stelios Haji-Ioannou, have family resources to fund their initiative, but most lack sufficient funds to take their enterprise from concept to take-off. Bank finance is inappropriate for startups, and bank lending is always at 'arms length' from the risks of the enterprise. Entrepreneurs depend largely on risk capital from venture capitalists or 'business angels', who share the risks of the enterprise and frequently wish to share in its direction.

Raising equity is difficult for entrepreneurs unless they have a history of successful innovation. Serial entrepreneurs frequently fail to replicate earlier success in later ventures, particularly in technology-based enterprises, though there are some exceptions, such as Professor Hopper of Cambridge, who has been consistently successful since his creation of Olivetti Research in 1986. Even Professor Hopper complains of a 'lack of traction' between earlier success and funding new deals. There would seem to be a need for a national clearing house to document performance and facilitate the funding of new deals. It was the close relationship between entrepreneurs and risk financiers which created and sustained Silicon Valley – it was also that close relationship which suspended judgement on many 'Internet boom' deals in the late 1990s.

WORKING WITH OTHERS

Another constraint on entrepreneurs is the need to work with others. It is not easy for individuals driven by the compulsion to prove themselves to relate openly and even-handedly to others. Many entrepreneurs are impatient of discussion or criticism and seek the advice which they wish to receive. When they build teams to support their expansion, too many seek clones of themselves or employees with whom they feel comfortable. Charles Dunstone of The Carphone Warehouse (see Chapter 5) goes out of his way to build a team of strong-minded people who will challenge him and ensure that issues are thoroughly debated before decisions are taken. Entrepreneurs also need to face their mortality and provide for orderly succession – John Ritblat has not done this effectively at British Land, or Michael Green at Carlton.

Entrepreneurs are usually better at working with customers than colleagues. Peter Drucker sees the purpose of business to be winning customers, and few entrepreneurs find this a difficult concept. It is more difficult for them to share the process of directing their business. This may be seen in many family companies where the founder wishes to extend his or her grip on the business and perpetuate his or her influence through employing family members in key roles. Rupert Murdoch has taken this objective to considerable lengths and has largely been successful in his entrepreneurial drive. Whether his relationship with colleagues has been equally successful is less clear.

Entrepreneurs and powerful chief executives share a problem with the concept of non-executive directors. Tiny Rowland filled the Lonrho board with pliant non-executive directors; Ken Morrison refused to appoint any at Morrisons Supermarkets until his bid for Safeway. Among smaller companies, non-executive directors are relatively few in number and many of those are family members or professional advisers. With the advent of the Higgs Report, requiring quoted companies to have a majority of non-executives on their board, there is increasing pressure to appoint them. Unfortunately few companies know how to use them effectively and will seek harmony on the board rather than encourage challenge.

POWER AND PUBLICITY

One of the basic tenets of corporate governance is the diffusion of power. Where power is concentrated it leads, so Lord Acton tells us, to corruption. A key feature of the Cadbury Code was the separation of the roles of chairperson and chief executive. This should ensure that the board is directed separately from the company so that power is divided at the top, encouraging its diffusion within the company to those who need to exercise it. This is the principle of 'subsidiarity', at the core of building the European Union, which seeks to ensure that power is exercised at as low a level as practicable. For many entrepreneurs, sharing power conflicts with the intensely personal nature of their mission. Delegation requires confidence and trust in others; most entrepreneurs see themselves as the key risk-takers in their enterprise and feel compelled to exercise close personal control of its development. This compulsion can be seen in the manoeuvrings of Paul Reichmann in developing a protecting control of Canary Wharf.

Some entrepreneurs are concerned to exploit publicity in building their businesses; in earlier days they usually put their name over the door, but this is now done less frequently (possibly because of the need nowadays to raise finance and involve others). Sir Clive Sinclair, the serial inventor, put his name to his various products – the failure of his C5 personal vehicle destroyed his business and his reputation. Most outgoing entrepreneurs now focus on creating brands which are associated with them but can stand separately. Microsoft is identified with Bill Gates, yet he puts his name only on his charitable undertakings. Brands can survive transfer and mortality – who is aware of the history of Elizabeth Arden or Louis Vuitton?

Other entrepreneurs tend to share publicity. Leo Kirch built his media business surreptitiously and lost it through secret deals. The Bronfman family built their empire with minimum publicity – young Edgar Bronfman Junior has lost much of it *con molto brio*. Publicity implies accountability; for many entrepreneurs accountability is solely between them and God.

LEADERSHIP

The success of entrepreneurs is crucially dependent on leadership. Since entrepreneurs are active by nature it might be thought that leadership was at the core of their being. Leadership is not, however, defined solely by ambitions – it manifests itself primarily in achieving results.

Many entrepreneurs show considerable ambition – Jean Marie Messier demonstrated an almost Napoleonic drive to build a global business empire out of the Compagnie Générale des Eaux. His failure to engage his colleagues in his undertaking, and the egocentric nature of his leadership, made his ambitions unrealisable. Leaders who have no followers are unlikely to produce results.

How should entrepreneurs demonstrate leadership? Few entrepreneurs can achieve their goals single-handedly; progress depends on debating the means of achieving those goals with others whose support is essential for success, without compromising on the goals themselves. Leadership requires a clear sense of direction and a shared commitment to move in that direction. In practice it is usually easier to agree on the ends to be achieved than on the means of doing so. Leadership is about building ownership of the process by which ends are achieved – sharing this is easier and more productive than compromising on goals, which no true entrepreneur can do.

RISK

Entrepreneurs are fascinated by risk. They are motivated to achieve what most people see as unachievable – to do so they have to venture into the unknown and take risks whose nature and extent are unknowable in advance. Entrepreneurs share motivation with explorers – they seek out new challenges which involve discomfort and risk in order to prove themselves to themselves. Risk is stimulating but needs to be controlled to maintain good governance. Many entrepreneurs are tempted to gamble – Calisto Tanzi of Parmalat seems to have over-reached himself with derivatives to protect other family interests.

The gambling instinct which is strong in so many entrepreneurs points to the need for countervailing measures of good governance to be maintained. Balance is a feature of good governance so that entrepreneurs need to understand their motivations and guard against excess. Having colleagues with different mindsets and complementary skills can help entrepreneurs to temper their own fantasies. It is usually assumed that bringing entrepreneurs together in intellectual hot houses stimulates creativity and engenders positive competition between them. This can lead to excessive innovation in which new initiatives are not properly evaluated or developed, leading to financial and reputational losses. While many entrepreneurs are stimulated by external competition, born entrepreneurs are mainly competing with themselves.

ENTREPRENEURS AND GOVERNANCE

How far do entrepreneurs work with or against the grain of corporate governance? At one extreme an entrepreneur behaves like a pirate, pushing his or her idea to the detriment of any other consideration. British traders stole rubber plants from Brazil to create their own rubber industry; other British traders forced the development of the opium market in China. Most entrepreneurs are not criminal or driven primarily by the desire for riches; many are like John Harrison, the clockmaker who struggled for many years to perfect the measurement of longitude with little financial backing. Frank Whittle went through purgatory to ensure that the jet engine could be realised. In both cases their success came despite establishment opposition – an establishment which set the rules of governance at the time!

The rules of governance inevitably reflect the values of the society which sets them. Deregulation is normal in emerging and changing societies, since entrepreneurs need encouragement to create wealth and build the economy. Regulation comes at the stage when some entrepreneurs are beginning to exercise monopoly power and/or seek political influence. This was seen in the early twentieth century with the breaking up of the US trusts; more recently the Russian oligarchs have suffered a form of regulation. Entrepreneurs' 'animal spirits' are essential for economic progress but the rest of society would prefer that they were domesticated.

ENTREPRENEURS AND NOLAN

By contrasting entrepreneurial characteristics, as shown in BusinessTown.com's 'Profile of an Entrepreneur' (Appendix A) with the Nolan principles, the problem of accommodating entrepreneurs within a corporate governance framework becomes evident:

Entrepreneurial characteristics	*Nolan*
Self-control	Accountability
Self-confidence	Leadership
Sense of urgency	
Comprehensive awareness	Integrity
Realism	Objectivity
Conceptual ability	
Status requirements	Selflessness
Interpersonal relationships	Openness
Emotional stability	
	Honesty

Corporate governance has been developed to referee team games; entrepreneurs prefer solo sports and compete primarily with themselves. Hence accountability and openness run counter to the entrepreneur's focus on self. Honesty does not even fit the picture – what entrepreneur will recognise any conflict of interest in meeting his or her goals? The main hope of channelling the drive of entrepreneurs into activities which are socially acceptable is to develop principles of governance which are not too prescriptive but which focus on openness and accountability. Entrepreneurs are part of society and need to respect its norms.

A 'comply or explain' approach to governance should meet the reasonable needs of entrepreneurs. Sir Ken Morrison of Morrisons Supermarkets does not meet many of the requirements of the Combined Code but his annual report explains his reasons for not doing so. If entrepreneurs – for example, those experimenting with cloning and other sensitive medical procedures – seek to hide their activities, it is now increasingly difficult to do so in a world of increasingly complex relationships. Entrepreneurs need capital, staff and specialist services, whose providers are themselves increasingly accountable to their own stakeholders. Recent provisions to support 'whistle-blowing' make it more difficult for conspiracies to be sustained.

A NEW APPROACH

More important for accommodating entrepreneurs to corporate governance is the need to move corporate governance from a 'box-ticking' examination to an open process of building trust. Corporate governance is only a means towards the end of enabling different parties to work together with confidence; the real proof of success is a business with sustainable growth. Growth is at the heart of entrepreneurialism, so that entrepreneurs need to be encouraged, sustained and rewarded for success but only on condition that they work openly with other stakeholders and share the burdens and excitement of building the business with them. To do so means sharing power and recognising the contribution of others to success – could Adrian Cadbury have been thinking of entrepreneurs when he pressed for the separation of the roles of chairperson and chief executive in his code?

Institute of Family Business

The Institute for Family Business (IFB) was founded in 2001 as an independent 'not for profit' organisation and it mission is to sustain a successful family business community in the UK, making a powerful contribution to the national economy. One of its role models is the German 'Mittelstand', the group of small and medium-sized businesses which comprise the core of the German economy. Hermann Simon's book *Hidden Champions* focuses on the 500 least known of these successful companies and analyses the secrets of their prosperity. Key to this prosperity is long termism; family companies are managed for long tenure, not necessarily managed by the family, but embedded in the family psyche. Family companies represent a significant concentration of wealth and need to be nurtured over generations.

Grant Gordon, Director General of the IFB, explained how his organisation helps to strengthen the family business sector of the economy. It operates as a network for its members who own and direct its activities. It offers regular networking opportunities for members and a range of educational programmes. It also sponsors research into family business and operates as the UK Chapter of the worldwide Family Business Network. The IFB is supported in its research and educational work by London Business School and is partnered with BDO Centre for Family Business.

In the same way that a growing number of Mittelstand firms are being sold, for example, Wella to Procter and Gamble, there has also been a decline in the number of family firms in the UK during the last two decades. Growing competition and government bureaucracy have tilted the balance between family commitment and the temptation of realising the value of family businesses. Firms like Weetabix have sold out and the importance of proper governance within the family, and separately for the business, is emerging strongly. IFB has found that the Family Business Honours, sponsored by JP Morgan Private Bank (see below) have helped to focus companies on the pursuit of excellence. Effective corporate governance is the key instrument for developing and sustaining excellence.

Families are realising that they can continue as owners of their companies only by separating direction from ownership. Succession is becoming a thorny issue for many family companies both due to the demand for talent to run businesses competitively and to the growing number of scions who have independent plans for their lives. Managerial skills are not always inherited and today's skills differ from those in the genes of the founder.

A recent survey by IFB showed that 25 per cent of members did not see their business being family directed in the future. Fewer family members now felt wedded to the family company – a few even saw it as a lifestyle provider which was unlikely to prosper.

Families with family councils tend to have better governance in the business also. There are clear rules and processes, and openness and accountability are required of all family members. Companies increasingly bring in outsiders to hold key posts, even that of CEO, and family members are expected to learn business skills and develop a track record outside the company before applying to join. Even then, the best ones offer no favours. IFB holds seminars on 'professionalising the board' which demonstrate the importance of the chairperson's role in developing and leading the board in the interests of the company, not of the family. Greater emphasis is laid on selecting and using non-executive directors, although only larger companies do so at present. The independence of non-executive directors is still untested in most companies; at Stakis the non-executives forced the resignation of the owner's son, but this is a benchmark, not common practice. In too many family companies, members of the family sit in the boardroom as shareholders, not directors. Keeping the family agenda out of the board room is a key role for non-executive directors, where the chairperson fails to do so. Fortunately most IFB member companies have non-executive directors and IFB offers good training for them.

The better family companies now have clear roles about entry by family members and about dovetailing generations of the family. There are also rules about family members reporting to non-family directors (this is often excellent for their personal development). Samworth Brothers and C & J Clark are directed by non-family members and this may be a growing trend. There is also a move towards diluting family control of equity. This often brings greater discipline, particularly where institutional investors are involved. The degree of dilution is a sensitive issue – too much interference from a disconnected minority family shareholding (Sainsbury's?) may be counter productive.

Corporate governance in family companies is in transition. The best companies, like Clark and William Jackson, have excellent governance and strong non-executives to coach family members. S C Johnson won a FBN award for corporate governance. The need for good governance is greater than ever as the life cycles of family companies contract. Many family businesses are started by entrepreneurs who are focused on innovation but less concerned with maturing and conserving their creations. This makes their business unstable and concentrates power in their hands. To be sustainable, businesses need a more stable structure with power dispersed and subject to challenge. Entrepreneurial businesses can become family businesses through the process of building families down the generations but this usually dilutes the 'animal spirits' which created the firm in the beginning. One of the challenges for IFB is to sustain and recreate the entrepreneurial skills which are often the key differentiator between family businesses and companies controlled by institutional shareholders.

Speculating about the future of family businesses, Grant Gordon saw the possibility of shorter life cycles, as family commitment was weakened by the need for increasing investment to meet competitive pressures and the temptation to realise profits early to feed lifestyles outside business. The conflict between family agendas and the interests of other stakeholders was likely to increase so that many family companies would evolve into enterprises with a dispersed ownership. Despite these changes, Grant saw the birth of new businesses as assured by the desire of entrepreneurial spirits to 'own their own show' and to share the benefits with their family. Family business was likely to be less monolithic in the future but family nurture would be of increasing importance as a stage in the development of successful world-class companies in the UK, many of which would choose to retain their family image. For many customers the family brand is a token of commitment and quality.

Family businesses

Family businesses are one of the major mainstays of the British economy. Most businesses are founded by entrepreneurs or by individuals with a personal mission; many of these fail within a few years due to misfortune, mismanagement or lack of funding. Of those which survive a significant number become family businesses when the founder marries and extends the horizon of his or her ambitions. According to Sir Adrian Cadbury (*Family Firms and their Governance* – Egon Zehnder International, 2000) the proportion of family firms among registered companies is estimated to be 75 per cent in the UK, ranging to over 95 per cent in India and other emerging markets. Family firms are believed to employ 50 per cent of people working in the UK private sector. Although the larger family firms are registered companies, the majority are partnerships or unincorporated enterprises. The contribution of family firms to Gross National Product (GDP) is very significant and there is some evidence that they are more resilient than the generality of businesses to internal and external shocks.

How do family businesses differ from other enterprises? There are many individual differences which are too specific to offer general patterns, but some key generic differences appear to be that:

- family businesses are owned rather than treated as an investment;
- families own their businesses for the long term and as an inheritance for successors;
- families tend to grow their businesses organically rather than by acquisition; and
- family businesses are funded and run conservatively in order to maintain control.

These characteristics are more pronounced in wholly owned family businesses. Where family control is watered down by partial flotation or following a merger, the family loses total control and needs to accommodate other stakeholders.

OWNERSHIP

The attraction of founding a business is to win independence from employers and the freedom to live and work for your own satisfaction. Many founders are surprised to find how their business takes over their lives and constrains their freedom. The daily routine of 'mom and pop' shops is unrelenting, marginalising holidays and hobbies, yet those involved cling to a hard lifestyle in order to build ownership. In effect they become the business and its life is their life. Even as a family business grows the obligations of ownership persist, so that family decisions are made in the light of the impact on the business (much as the landowner lives for his estate). When family businesses mature and members of the family have more day-to-day freedom in their lives, the business remains at the centre of the family consciousness and shapes their major decisions.

Ownership is the cement which binds family members to their business. Often it is reinforced by the opportunity for some members of the family to work in the business. Sometimes family members are expected to work in the business and this can lead to frustration, where ambitions lie elsewhere, or to exploitation, where the member is seen as cheap labour. The effect of living and working together as a family can be claustrophobic and business issues can spill over into family life. Maintaining ownership beyond two generations is difficult for families and the health of the business depends on the quality of family members. The spirit and skill of the founder may not be reproduced down the line. The saying: 'Clogs to clogs in three generations', in which the first generation founds the business, the second builds it and the third dissipates it, is true of too many family firms, particularly when they fail to distinguish ownership from management and do not seek the best external talent to run the business.

LONG-TERM VIEW

Where family businesses are not answerable to external investors it is easier to take a long-term view about profitability. Quarterly reporting has been very damaging for many quoted companies and makes long-term investment appear unattractive. Family companies, with an eye to inheritance and succession, are more likely to accept lower returns over an extended period than a company answerable to institutional investors. Morrison's Supermarkets has built its business out of organic growth (until the recent take-over of Safeway) generated by consistently low prices; Sainsbury's (still a minority family company) has tried to trade in the premium zone of food retailing without having the cachet of Waitrose, in order to generate high profits and dividends. Morrison's has prospered for some 60 years; Sainsbury's has lost market share to Tesco and Asda and is a fading force in UK retailing.

A significant phenomenon in building family businesses is the German 'Mittelstand'. This is the block of medium-sized businesses, largely founded after 1945 on the back of the Marshall Plan which has been the driving force of the German economy until recent years. These businesses have been based in Germany and most have traded globally. Few are quoted companies; most have been, until recently, family controlled. Their ability to take a long view of investment has enabled them to build markets patiently. Some have used bank finance to fund expansion and German banks have been supportive until the recent recession. After 50 odd years these companies which have largely been impregnable to take-over are beginning to sell out. In many cases, this is due to a weakening of family commitment, but the high cost of manufacturing in Germany and cheaper overseas competition has affected a large number. A typical case is that of Wella, the hair products group, sold to Procter and Gamble, which is still subject to litigation from smaller shareholders.

The long-term view seems to support company growth for anything up to 50 years – this coincides eerily with the third generation in 'clogs to clogs'!

ORGANIC GROWTH

Family businesses have a strong ethos of ownership which implies a known culture and effective control. Serial entrepreneurs, such as Stelios Hani-Ioannou and Richard Branson, are driven by ideas rather than control and their approach differs fundamentally from that of most family businesses. Entrepreneurs work for themselves; family companies work for their inheritance. Both, however, tend to favour organic growth over acquisitions – entrepreneurs need to create businesses out of their own ideas; families focus on ownership.

Mergers and acquisitions are for businesspeople in a hurry. They provide instant growth and feed the ego of the acquiring CEO. They bring alien cultures into the group and often bring hidden risks – neither are attractive to entrepreneurs or family businesses. (It remains to be seen whether Morrison's has over-reached itself or whether it is metamorphosing into a non-family business.)

CONSERVATIVE FUNDING

The low cost of borrowing in recent years has led many major companies to invest heavily in bonds and debentures to the point where many have higher debt than equity. Many of these companies have also been cutting dividends in order to force growth, alienating investors but promising future capital growth. Family firms are unlikely to indulge in such behaviour, both because they seek controllable organic growth and because they behave as owners.

Family companies focus largely on equity to fund their business. They issue enough shares to support organic growth and they may not pay a dividend for some years until their company is safely afloat. In later years they will pay a dividend which meets the needs of the family and avoids excessive tax. The cash needs of the business are usually funded from retained profits, supplemented by short-term overdrafts as necessary. Some family firms have used debt instruments in recent years but this is usually small relative to their equity.

INCREASING FOCUS ON FAMILY BUSINESSES

Despite the importance of the family business sector to the UK economy, it has until recently been neglected by government and by educators. Family businesses usually have a low profile, unless there is trouble, and their activities are not well-monitored statistically. The steady concentration of quoted companies into amorphous groups (often with confusing names) has led to a growing interest in smaller companies and an increase in research by analysts into their potential. At the same time a growing number of quoted companies are becoming unlisted through buyouts – DFS Furniture is the latest to make this move back to family control – so that the Stock Exchange is no longer the sole focus of interest for observers of the British economy. To stimulate this interest further and to encourage greater appreciation of the merits of family companies, Mark Evans, Vice President of JP Morgan Private Bank, conceived a new programme to focus interest on family business. In 2003 the Bank launched its 'UK Family Business Honours Programme'. This programme is supported by the Institute for Family Business and London Business School (LBS) and its awards are open to family companies which have reached at least the third generation of family ownership. The programme for 2003 was supported by Patricia Hewitt, Secretary of State at the DTI.

Criteria for judging the awards, which are evaluated by independent panels for each of three areas of best practice (family governance, business success and social responsibility) include, in respect of family governance:

- A clearly articulated statement of mission and values which guide the family and its business
- A family council, constitution or other mechanism for conducting family governance
- Succession plans or processes regarding ownership and leadership transition
- An effective process for communications and conflict management
- A successful policy for the integration of family and non-family management.

There are different criteria for the business success and social responsibility awards.

In 2003, 18 firms were honoured under the three areas of best practice as follows:

- For family governance

Exemplar	– C & J Clark Ltd	(footwear)
Others	– C Hoare & Co	(bankers)
	– Thomas Crosbie Holdings Ltd	(publishers)
	– William Jackson and Son Ltd	(foods)
	– J W Lees & Co (Brewers) Ltd	(beer)
	– Perfecta Ltd	(spices and seasonings)
	– Speymalt Whisky Distributors	(whisky)

- For business success

Exemplar	– Samworth Brothers	(food)
Others	– Altro Group plc	(wall and ceiling systems)
	– Big Pictures	(photographic publishers)
	– Grosvenor Group Holdings Ltd	(international property)
	– Lornamead International	(home and personal care products)
	– The Musgrove Group	(food distribution)
	– Thomas Crosbie Holdings Ltd	(publishers)
	– Timpson	(shoe and other repairs)

- For social responsibility

Exemplar	– Betty's and Taylors of Harrogate	(food, food retailing)
Other	– Bruntwood Estates	(commercial property)
	– C Hoare and Co	(bankers)
	– IMO Precision Controls Ltd	(automation and electronic components)
	– Pentland Group plc	(sports fashions)
	– Samworth Brothers	(food)

This list shows the variety among family companies and their ability to exploit interesting and profitable niches in various markets by distinguishing themselves. The LBS report on the programme for 2003 shows how different is each of these businesses from other award recipients, not only in market orientation, but in style and character. The judges were impressed by the quality of nominated firms and by the scale and depth of their presentations. The nominees represent only a sample of family businesses in Britain, so that it must be supposed that future programmes will draw forth candidates of at least equal merit. (The 2004 programme has done so.)

GOVERNANCE IN FAMILY COMPANIES

Family companies raise issues of corporate governance, some of which have been mentioned earlier, which challenge the basic concept of balancing power which makes governance effective. Families need to separate the worlds of home and business in order to lay the foundations for good governance of their company. This has the following elements:

- Governing the family
- Opening the company to wider influence
- Providing for orderly growth and control
- Ensuring continuity.

Let us examine these elements in further detail:

Governing the family

Sir Adrian Cadbury sees 'every merit in providing a clear and accepted structural division between the governance of the firm and the deliberations of the family'. His approach to governing the family is to establish a family forum in which family and business issues may be discussed. Membership criteria need to be settled, probably linked to shareholding but also involving younger members of the family of an appropriate age. Because of the implications for all members of the council's deliberations, it is recommended that its proceedings be orderly and recorded. Sir Adrian Cadbury even suggests that the forum be managed by members who are not involved in the company and that the family views on issues be communicated to the company solely via the forum.

Most families with control of a business have mechanisms for developing career options for younger members. These keep them informed about the family business but open other options so that their choice is informed and personal. Sometimes family members have interests outside the business – Geoffrey Tate (of Tate and Lyle) became a famous conductor (shades of Beecham!). Whatever process is adopted its main purpose in respect of corporate governance is to insulate the company from family rivalries or undue influence.

Where companies are wholly family owned it may be advisable to establish a trust to own all the shares. This avoids the danger of split shareholdings and ensures perpetual control, but does require the appointment of independent trustees. The Wellcome Trust was an example of such an arrangement, some of which are established offshore, for example, Vestey.

Opening the company to wider influence

One fundamental problem with family businesses is their tendency to encourage intro-spection. Too many find employing people other than family members inhibiting, either because it reduces work opportunity for those in the family or because it constrains communication at work between family members. Family businesses tend to have inhibitions in external contacts, particularly if there are family ties to professional advisers or key suppliers. This tendency to introspection is a key reason for isolating the business from family concerns.

How should family companies open up to wider influences? There are many facets to this issue and it may be useful to address it in parts.

Shareholding

Many family companies seek external shareholders only to fund the development of their business. This is logical, but it makes sense also to invite external shareholding from individuals or groups who can bring a wider perspective to the business and its development. Some of these may become non-executive directors, but others may offer specialist insight on contacts which are beyond the knowledge of family members. As long as the total external shareholding is less than 25 per cent, the family retains effective control of the business; in practice, if external shareholdings are well dispersed, a family holding of 50 per cent plus is sufficient. It was at one time common for different classes of share to be issued to focus control on families. This device is now more frequently used in Switzerland and other European countries and is not favoured by the Stock Exchange. The *Daily Mail and General Trust* still has two share classes, and some unquoted companies have weighted voting rights, but the practice is disappearing over time in the UK.

If the family company is very successful it has the option to float 20 per cent or more of its shares on the Stock Exchange. This takes it beyond the point where most shareholders are known individually and will raise its profile with the media and a wider circle of investors. There are a number of quoted companies where families have significant influence even with a shareholding as low as 20 per cent, due to the pattern of holding within the majority, for example, Sainsbury's. At some point the family influence becomes largely symbolic and the company is truly public.

The board of directors

Family companies are frequently tempted to limit board appointments to family members. This is a bad practice, both because it potentially confuses company issues and family issues but also because it misses the opportunity to bring wider knowledge and experience to handle company affairs. Companies should never use board appointments as trophies in the competition between family members, nor should family issues ever be aired at board meetings.

Few families have in their ranks all of the skills needed to direct a company in the modern era. The wiser ones recognise that company performance can only be sustained by appointing directors who will make a significant contribution to the business. Where there are external shareholders the need to avoid any nepotism on the board is increased, since external shareholders are likely to expect a higher economic performance from the company and a board capable of delivering it.

Many family businesses open their board membership initially to non-family non-executive directors as a way of experimenting with external influence on their company. This is a model favoured by Adrian Cadbury since non-executive directors take time to familiarise themselves with the details of company business and their learning process eases the discomfort of sharing private information with outsiders. Use of external non-executive directors also reduces in some measure the need to use external advisers. Some family companies establish advisory boards to provide advice without exercising power. Few such initiatives have been successful and it is difficult to attract effective people for a passive role.

Family companies really 'come of age' when they appoint external executive directors. The post of finance director is frequently the first external appointment, since there may be no accountants in the family. Some companies deal with this issue by appointing a former auditor as a non-executive director and inviting the financial controller to sit in and report at board meetings. This is not a good solution for a pivotal appointment. Appointing an external chief executive is the key step in taking a company out of the family ambit into the wider world. Sometimes this is preceded by appointing an external managing director to deliver the strategy decided by the board with policy power controlled by an executive chairperson from the family. However the goal of separating ownership from control is achieved, it is for many companies the moment when their destiny is liberated from family constraints without losing the culture and values which make them distinctive.

Other stakeholders

Employees are key stakeholders in a family company. Many people will not work for a family business as they fear discrimination in promotion opportunities. Others are attracted by family companies because of their culture and values. At one time family companies were often seen as 'paternalistic', building company estates like Bournville or Port Sunlight and shaping the lives of employees. This view has faded, not least because some family companies, due to Quaker or other values, have sought to protect employment in times of recession.

Family companies are sensitive today to the need to avoid any hint of discrimination in making appointments. While few refuse to allow family members to work for them, it is becoming accepted practice for appointments to be subject to competitive interview with external monitoring. Many companies are now requiring family members to work initially outside the firm and to seek employment only when they have an established record of success. It seems likely that the pattern of recruiting family members into the company on leaving school will not survive, since increasingly members will wish to go to university and will have their horizons extended in the process. Young family members are less willing to work in the family firm for low wages in the hope of a secure future when they are older.

Other key stakeholders in family companies are customers. For smaller companies these are often known personally to the family and may sometimes be friends. Such relationships need to be set in a business-like context if a clash between personal links and business relations is to be avoided. Many small companies have been damaged by family friends who are bad payers. On the other hand the reputation of family companies is often attractive to customers, who welcome the consistency and continuity offered by family companies and pass their loyalty down the generations. Family boards are often reinforced by family values, for example Hoare, the banker. Weetabix resisted the might of Kellogg and other mega-competitors for many years due to its wholesome reputation. Purdey, the gun maker, was sold to Richemont, which has retained Richard Purdey as Managing Director, in order to preserve the value of its family brand.

Suppliers are important to family companies for the ideas they bring as much as for merchandise. Lengthening supply chains make supplier relations increasingly important and suppliers respond to the continuity and values usually associated with family companies. Companies like Betty's and Taylors source worldwide and value their reputation for fair dealing.

Communities are important to family companies which have a strong 'sense of place'. The roots of family companies often dig deeply and within the close relationships with communities which are typical of them. It is for this reason that entries in the 'JP Morgan Private Bank Family Business Honours' do well in the assessment of corporate social responsibilities. Family companies are also prominent in Business in the Community and in support for charities, particularly those local to the company. Family companies are often very important in their local area, which sometimes restricts their ability to move operations. The transfer of manufacture overseas by Dyson, the vacuum cleaner company, was heavily resented locally and has tarnished their image. Learning to expand out of their core community is a challenge for developing family businesses. Some family companies never grow or leave their roots – one such is a small building company in Kent, Dartnell and Co, which was founded in the sixteenth century.

Growth and control

For family companies, growth is usually a function of meeting family needs rather than a reaction to external pressure or personal ambition. Families favour stability and limited risk in the companies they own, and are concerned to pass to the next generation a business which is in good health. To provide this health and steady growth, family companies are heavily reliant on managing the expectations of family members and protecting the business from greed or incompetence. This process is best managed outside the company through a family forum or equivalent.

Within the company, corporate governance focuses on the mission set for it by its controlling shareholders (the family), and the directors have less freedom of action than those of a normal limited company. This constraint can be frustrating to external directors and shareholders but diminishes as the balance of power moves towards external shareholders. Family caution may cause companies to miss new opportunities, but may also rescue them from perils, for example Saga Holidays has been more consistent than other travel companies (and sold out for one billion pounds recently).

Where family companies introduce external shareholders or directors, extra care is needed to open an ongoing dialogue with them and to ensure that all governance processes are completely open. External executive directors must be given space to work effectively, not hampered by family member manoeuvres. Fairness is a key touchstone in all dealings with outside parties and all transactions must be open. Family companies which earn a reputation for family favouritism can rarely secure the services of good employees and have tainted relations with other stakeholders. Where families are seen to be fair in their external dealings, their companies usually prosper.

The future of family companies

It is a very healthy paradox that the concentration of companies into ever larger groups leads to increased spawning of small companies. Most of these are started by entrepreneurs or groups of entrepreneurs and many of those which survive become family companies, linked to a controlling shareholder. Family companies founded by groups of siblings are now fewer, due in part to the fragility of families, but small shops and service businesses continue to follow the 'mom and pop' tradition. Mark Evans of JP Morgan Private Bank believes passionately in the value of family companies and in their future prospects. He sees the best of them as exemplars for improving British business: 'By identifying best practice in family firms we are also creating role models for the entire business community.' He believes that family businesses are underevaluated and that they can be encouraged to adopt a higher profile and counter the negative image which larger businesses have attracted. He also emphasises the spirit of innovation which emanates from the best family businesses which see themselves as creators and developers of key market niches. Such businesses are capable of coping with change and some even drive it.

The Internet is gradually changing the dynamics of business, so that for some, location is less important than price. Building trust over the Internet remains an unresolved challenge and trust is strong in family business. The Internet offers wide choice and keen prices yet lacks the empathy which stimulates good business. It is likely that we shall see major efforts to build 'Internet brands', so that remoteness is offset by confidence in the brand. Amazon, eBay and others are striving to build brands but this is not a process which can be achieved in a few years. Brands like Clarks have taken nearly 200 years to grow, so we may see a move by Internet companies to buy established brands to win time.

Family companies depend on the power of heritage to motivate their owners to fight for a sustainable niche in a competitive world. Families are less united today than in the past, and family members less patient, yet markets will probably make space for businesses which are idiosyncratic and interesting and which have healthy values and a long-term approach to profitability. Most of us like to deal with others we see as similar to ourselves – family companies have the same concern for their children and basic decency which we seek in our own lives. It will always be more comforting to deal with them than with mega corporations or faceless websites.

7 Reputation and Social/ Ecological Responsibility

Social and ecological responsibility are currently touchstones for corporate reputation. I believe that this is a fashion and that reputation is both deeper and wider than these individual concerns. It is likely that they will be subsumed into the larger issue of reputation but will remain important elements in the mix.

Reputation – a view from Stewart Lewis, Director of MORI Ltd

Stewart Lewis sees reputation as the totality of the emotional and intellectual disposition of individuals and groups towards another organisation. Reputation is both seen and felt, and becomes the identity of that organisation in the eyes of others. Reputation is more than a brand, although branding is subsumed into reputation, particularly at corporate level. Reputation depends on the economic performance of the organisation and its product brands but is distilled into a deeper level of trust. Branding is focused on what the company sells; reputation reflects what it stands for.

The search for ways to build reputation has taken many companies into the realm of corporate social responsibility (CSR). This has been led usually by public relations people and has sometimes suffered from a mismatch between image and reality. Stewart is convinced that CSR can only be effective if it involves the whole company. CSR requires integrity to be sustainable so that the image projected must be consistent at all levels, much as the text in a stick of Brighton rock goes from end to end. Stewart tells the story of a journalist who doubted the integrity of BP's CSR until a junior technician insisted that it really was 'the way we all work'. CSR needs to be embedded in daily operations to be effective over time – there is no short cut to building a sustainable reputation.

Stewart sees multiple threats to corporate reputation. Shell management seems to have tolerated misreporting of reserves in order to sustain its market ranking. Where were the famous 'checks and balances' which built Shell's reputation for integrity? Shell's new structure will hopefully restore its internal controls and remove impediments to its future success. Boeing seems to have suffered from a corrupt employee 'cutting corners' in order to win business. Massive corruption seriously damaged the reputation of Elf Acquitaine some years ago.

Big contracts in secretive markets are a moral hazard which faces defence and construction companies worldwide – the reputation of Halliburton has been tarnished by its performance in Iraq. Failure to maintain the confidence of customers destroyed the market leadership of Marks & Spencer. Too many companies lose touch with their stakeholders and become internally focused. The 'new formula' of Coca-Cola was developed and marketed without serious consultation with customer groups. Reputation is awarded or withdrawn by others; it is not in our own gift but we can work to enhance and sustain it.

How can companies recover their reputation after a mishap? To do so requires a residual fund of goodwill on which to build (totally lacking in the case of Arthur Andersen). Many of the US companies tainted by scandal, for example, MCI and Tyco, are moving from intensive care towards recovery, aided by a complete change of management and vigorous surgery. The other key factor identified by Stewart Lewis is the need for full and frank communication. Perrier failed to admit its quality problem until its reputation was severely damaged. Johnson & Johnson reacted fast with Tylenol contamination and maintained goodwill. Stewart sees the ability to apologise frankly as powerful in a world where 'sorry' is no longer in the dictionary. This ability to say 'sorry' (as with Johnson & Johnson) is crucial – but is no part of 'PR speak'. In a world of labyrinthine call centres, some enterprising insurers and other service businesses are rediscovering the power of letters of apology in differentiating themselves from their unthinking competitors. An enhanced will to listen to customers and other stakeholders is crucial in order to recover reputation. Improved communications has helped the new management of Equitable Life to stabilise the society and prevent self-destructive litigation. The new management of Marconi has won increasing support from the City and other stakeholders through communicating commitments and steadily delivering them. Stewart Lewis recognises that it takes some fifty years on average to build a solid reputation but he believes that, where there is residual goodwill after a disaster, recovery may be well advanced after two years.

The ownership of reputation is complex in Stewart's view. Shareholders own the company in legal terms and its reputation is reflected in share prices. Other stakeholders share in a company's reputation – employees like to work for a well-respected organisation, customers like to be associated with a supplier which echoes their good taste and judgement and suppliers like to deal with prestige accounts. Self-belief is, however, at the heart of reputation. External stakeholders respond to that self-belief, they rarely create it. Where it is undermined, as in the infamous comment by Gerald Ratner that his company sold 'crap', external support disappears rapidly. Self-belief also has to be based on a commitment to serve; companies which are used for exploitation by their legal owners, for example Parmalat and Hollinger, may project self-belief but have no meaningful agenda to build a sustainable reputation. As we have seen, reputation is accorded by others and invites a continuing relationship, but who would want a continuing relationship with Barlow Clowes?

Stewart Lewis sees the core of reputation management as being a choice of standards for performance and behaviour, sustained by constant external appraisal. Companies need to have a clear commitment to such standards which should be measurable and externally reviewed. All stakeholders need to be involved in the process which should be an ongoing conversation with all parties. The standards set should be challenging in order both to be competitive in the market place and to generate constantly better standards. This is analogous to the process established by Jack Walsh at GE, using Six-Sigma tools, but without over-personalisation. Stewart finds that many companies seek external support in building their reputation, not only with techniques and comparisons, but with objective advice. Companies can easily become complacent and need to understand their present and future vulnerabilities. The MORI Reputation Centre deals mainly with the Public Affairs/Corporate Communications department of their clients. I suggested that reputation was a board issue and was linked to strategy. Stewart agreed that top-level support was needed for the process of building reputation, in particular in ensuring that all parts of the business (and key stakeholders) were involved in it and that people were properly educated to make it work. Education in reputational risk and how to manage it was a key area of concern, not only to meet Turnbull reporting requirements but also to evaluate daily trade-offs. Many companies made routine decisions which threatened their reputation; the growth of call centres was an example of damaging reputation in the long term in order to save costs in the short term. Unless companies learned to put a value on their reputation it was difficult to make reasoned trade-offs. It was the claims department of some insurers, for example, Direct Line, which built their reputation.

We spoke about the value of intangible assets of which reputation was a substantial element for most companies. Interbrand had developed measures which had been accepted by accountants and some companies, for example, Skandia had started to put intangibles (other than goodwill of acquisitions) on their balance sheet. So far the process had not made great progress, since it raised wider questions of evaluating return on assets, volatility of valuations, and so on. Stewart felt that reputation management was built on relationships and that behaviours were the currency which sustained it. It was possible to measure reputation without use of financial reporting, although the requirement for an Operating and Financial Review in the new Companies Bill may call for quantified measures. At present MORI has a range of tools for evaluating a company's reputation which include reputation audits and reputation tracking. These tools are driven by systematic analysis, supported by the use of focus groups. MORI also has the MORI Excellence Model (MEM) which enables companies to rate their reputation on a scale from awareness through trust, transaction satisfaction and commitment to advocacy. This model also helps with stakeholder relationship analysis, another key tool for building reputation. A list of MORI reputation management tools is shown below.

In the view of Stewart Lewis, employee involvement is a key driver of reputation building. Employees interact with all stakeholders, often daily, and need to be motivated to act as ambassadors for the company. If employees are not so motivated it is unlikely that stakeholders will respond and create a value-creating relationship. BP sets the whole process in the context of sustainable development: 'To deliver the continuous improvement in performance and profitability that is our fundamental goal, we have to show we are a part of a process of sustainable development, beneficial to all' (Lord Browne, BP Annual Report 2001). BP talks continually with its employees to ensure that there is a clear line of sight to sustainable success. BP has four key brand values – innovative, progressive, performance driven, green – and behaviours to match them. Managers have rewards/sanctions linked to such behaviours and are appraised annually. Their performance is not geared to short-term success at the expense of future sustainability. Some people have been dismissed for failure to respect the values and BP now audits decisions in the light of results. Rio Tinto has emerged as a thought leader in reputation management. BAT has a set of business principles which are monitored at top level. Both are also active in local communities. Diageo is also active in managing its reputation (see Chapter 5).

Progress in improving reputation management depends less on pioneering companies, in the view of Stewart Lewis, than in overcoming fear and inertia among the rest. Some companies see reputation management, and in particular CSR, as the thin ends of a very threatening wedge. They see themselves becoming at the mercy of NGOs and other activists who will make unreasonable demands of them and divert their attention from developing their company. They are also nervous of the growing demands of government and the weight of bureaucracy. For companies who are focused on satisfying shareholders, a world in which they face multiple audiences is very threatening. I suggested to Stewart Lewis that a forum was needed in which different stakeholders and interested parties, such as government and media, could meet and debate how to build trust between them in an increasingly complex world. The organiser of that forum would need to be neutral and well informed – might MORI create and oversee such a forum?

Stewart Lewis sees reputation as having increasing importance for companies in crowded and competitive global markets. Buying and selling aggressively and primarily on price militates against longer-term relationships and increases the cost of acquisition often by an order of magnitude compared with working with known partners. An established reputation facilitates the contracting process and reduces the potential for misunderstanding and litigation. Trust is at the heart of such relationships, saving considerable cost and delay, so that contracts focus on essential issues and are made with confidence rather than fear.

MORI's Reputation Centre has more than 30 years' experience of working with companies and their stakeholders to build and sustain corporate reputation. MORI's clients for corporate reputation research include a wide cross-section of FTSE companies, some foreign businesses such as Ford, Microsoft, Nestlé, Nokia and Novartis, and organisations such as Royal Mail, the AA, the BBC and Camelot.

The centre's work focuses on the role of communication in building reputation. It addresses key questions, such as:

- What are your target audiences' greatest interests and concerns?
- How far are you seen to be meeting their expectations?
- How do you benchmark against your competitors for share of mind or awareness?
- Are you capitalising on your reputation strengths?
- Are you worrying about the wrong problems?
- How can your communications work best to build the reputation you seek?
- What media would be most suitable, and effective, to get your messages across?

These and other questions are addressed to representatives of key audiences and the results analysed in depth. Separate key audience research programmes cover government, media, business leaders and the City, and help to set focused research into a wider context.

MORI's main reputation management tools include:

- Reputation audits
- Reputation tracking
- Corporate identity, naming and branding
- Corporate social responsibility
- Elite focus groups
- Stakeholder relationship analysis (including the MORI Excellence Model)
- Multi-client surveys (the Key Audience Research Programme)
- Website evaluation (using e-MORI)
- International research.

The centre also produces key area research papers which help to shape the development of reputation management. Recent examples include:

- The rise and rise of non-financial reporting – how to use research to measure your reputation

- In search of lost trust
- The public's views of corporate responsibility 2003
- Focusing on the future of corporate governance
- Reputation and corporate responsibility.

Good Corporation – building an ethical company

One of the fundamental challenges of corporate governance is to shape the behaviours of employees from top to bottom of an organisation. Efforts to do this by 'corporate fiat' have never achieved sustainable results, since they rarely convince people's minds and never win their hearts. Another approach is that of the Good Corporation which seeks to agree and monitor standards for 'corporate responsibility' which focus on fairness rather than efficiency.

The Good Corporation was established in 2000 and launched in July 2001 by a group of former KPMG partners and directors, with support from the Institute of Business Ethics. Leo Martin is one of the founding directors and has overseen the building of the standard to a point of proven viability. The purpose of Good Corporation is to help businesses to establish and implement effective corporate responsibility practices throughout their organisation. The basic instrument for doing this is a well-tested standard which can be adapted for each organisation without losing the basic comparability between them all and the ability to award a 'Kitemark' or marque for success.

The process involves each organisation preparing evidence of good performance in each of its business units against each of 66 'practices', derived from 23 'principles'. There is a 70-page guidance manual to assist the preparation of the 'business case' from which the evaluation will be constructed and verified. Good Corporation has a list of consultants trained to assist in preparing submissions; as verifiers Good Corporation cannot offer consultancy services. The verification is undertaken by representatives of Good Corporation and will involve a 'bottom up' review in all business units and support functions, evaluating each in detail and awarding one of five grades for each 'practice'. These are in steps from 'fail', through 'minor non-compliance', 'observation' and 'merit' to 'commendation'. Each assessment is supported by copies of policy documents, system outputs, procedure manuals and interviews.

Once the individual reports have been synthesised, key issues are set out and an action plan for improvement is prepared for management. This report includes quality metrics for each 'practice', set against the Good Corporation benchmark. Where previous reviews have been done, the results of the latest review are compared with earlier ones to highlight any changes. Companies which have no fail grades across all 66 practices are entitled to use the Good Corporation marque; those who need some rectification will need to concentrate on improving the areas which score 'fail' gradings. In addition to scoring each organisation, Good Corporation benchmarks its scores against the average of all successful members.

Good Corporation verifies organisations of all types and size. Its members include global corporations such as Total and British Gas (BG) Group, specialist organisations such as FTSE, ARM Holdings, Ladbrokes and Classic FM, as well as Pensions Trust (which provides pension schemes for the voluntary sector) and LSTC, a trade union. Verifications are carried out worldwide and assist multi-national companies to ensure a consistency of behaviours across their operations which eludes most of their peers.

The purpose of the Good Corporation marque is both to distinguish members and help them to secure sales, and to ensure a consistency of behaviours which builds reputation and helps to avoid surprises. The results of the verification are confidential; only the marque is public and its use is controlled by the members. The Good Corporation does not seek to impose value judgements; its principles are those embraced by most successful businesses and its practices reflect behaviours which create trust and help to sustain performance.

The process involves all stakeholders of the organisation, internal and external, together with NGOs, protest groups and other potential critics. This helps to defuse actual and potential conflict and to build support for the organisation. The list of principles and practices is not exhaustive; some organisations may have practices which go beyond those which are benchmarked. Such extra features are brought into consideration but do not affect the overall rating.

Corporate governance is built into the process, both specifically in Practices SHA8 and 9, and by inference in most other 'practices'. The 65-page report produced by the verifiers is a powerful (but confidential) indicator of 'problems in the engine room' which can guide remedial action. It is no coincidence that some of the members have businesses all round the world and that the process can reveal weak spots in certain areas which may reflect a pattern of poor performance across countries or linked patterns of inadequacy across different activities within one business unit. At its worst this may be corruption, even fraud, but the process also picks up weakening performance in certain areas, compared with earlier verifications, which may be caused by bad appointments or by inadequate training or supervision. For a client like Total, with 200 subsidiaries worldwide and 130 000 employees, the task of verification and of ensuring consistency of assessment is daunting. With the need to ensure continuous improvement the task of verification resembles that of painting the Forth Bridge!

Good Corporation is commissioned by various client representatives. At Total the key client is a main board director, supported by the Ethics Committee. At BG the lead client is taken by Community Affairs; at Trinity Mirror, the Legal and Compliance Director leads; at ARM the HR Director is lead client and at DHL it is the Communications Director. The motivation for verification also varies. Risk minimisation is a frequent motive; another is the need for benchmarks for appraising employees. To date few members have been driven by a desire to improve their business results; most seem to see the standard as a defence mechanism, rather than as a lever to achieve outstanding results.

After three years Good Corporation has completed 100 verifications and has tested and calibrated its process. Its clientele has grown largely by chance and has no settled pattern. It is mainly in the private sector, with medium to large organisations, many of which have a high profile and a need to protect their reputation. The process would work equally well in the public sector but the need for it has yet to be recognised. Good Corporation sees its way forward by marching down the FTSE 100 Index into the 250 and beyond. There is already one major foreign client, and more will be sought, but care needs to be exercised to build the standard among organisations which are broadly comparable. Most importantly new clients will need to be willing to open all parts of their business to rigorous scrutiny and to treat the verification as a trigger for action. They will also need to have the patience and perseverance to allow their smallest and remotest business units to work out their own improvements in the context of the overall standard.

Business in the Community – social responsibility in practice

Business in the Community is well introduced by its website:

Business in the Community was set up in 1982 against a backdrop of enormously high levels of unemployment and urban rioting. Many observed that although large companies were beginning to play a key role in sponsoring major sporting and cultural events, companies in the United States were much more involved with their local communities than their British counterparts.

Sir Alastair Pilkington, who had previously set up the pathfinder Enterprise Agency in St Helens, was chosen to chair a new organisation promoting corporate community involvement. He thus became the Founder of Business in the Community, insisting from the outset that Business in the Community should be a genuine partnership between business, government, local authorities and trade unions.

Business in the Community opened its doors with a handful of valiant secondees to spread an uncertain message. Although a company chairman might agree that it was in his shareholders' interests to become involved in the community, it remained to be seen what he should do about it on Monday morning. The first answer lay with the enterprise agency movement, and the creation of this national network to 'hold the hand of new and developing business' became Business in the Community's first priority.

By 1985 the support network was nearly complete and there was convincing evidence that it vastly increased the life expectancy of new businesses.

Two years later, in 1987, HRH The Prince of Wales accepted the Presidency of Business in the Community. The Prince's unique ability to bring together and interpret the messages from depressed inner-city community groups as well as leaders from business and government has made him an outstanding leader of the community involvement movement for the past 16 years.

Business in the Community is a membership organisation limited by guarantee and a registered charity, operating in England, Wales and Northern Ireland. It is run within a business framework in pursuit of its purpose, which is defined in its Memorandum of Association. Business in the Community has 32 directors, all non-executive and unpaid, many from member companies. The CEO, Julia Cleverdon, is not on the board but runs her own management committee. Business in the Community runs a number of national campaigns the leaders of which are on its board. Business in the Community offers an umbrella for such campaigns and for the business initiatives which they engender. Business in the Community itself is funded by corporate members, most of whom are quoted on the London Stock Exchange.

As an expanding, project-led organisation, Business in the Community requires a broadly based board of non-executive directors to represent all its stakeholders. In order to provide operating focus, and support the management committee, David Varney has established a Chairman's Committee of 15 directors, overseeing key issues such as campaigns, projects, audit and nominations. There is a separate Finance and Audit Committee with five members, two of whom are directors. In addition to other duties this committee oversees budgeting and risk management (using Turnbull processes) and manages cash and debtors.

Julia Cleverdon, the CEO of Business in the Community, reports to the chairman, David Varney. Her key executive colleagues include a deputy CEO (for campaigns), a field director, a finance director, a HR director, a communications director and a company secretary: Business in the Community has a turnover of £17.5 million, although activities under its umbrella have considerably larger revenues. Business in the Community is an enabler not a holding company; its purpose is to inspire, challenge, engage and support business in continually improving its positive impact on society. Its role is to build a better society, through encouraging greater corporate social responsibility and helping to create more prosperous communities. Its method of operation is by changing and influencing business practice.

Business in the Community is not itself a social enterprise (as defined in the 2002 DTI White Paper) but is willing to include selected social enterprises under its umbrella. It remains a charity, as its board and members wish, but needs to exercise prudence in pursuing its social goals. Building reserves is a challenge for Business in the Community as it undertakes increasing commitments and risk.

Business in the Community is now 20 years old and has consulted with its stakeholders about its future objectives. These stakeholders include corporate sponsors, campaign groups, local communities, government, suppliers and its regulator, the Charity Commission, and its own employees. The outcome of this consultation will set the strategic agenda well into the future. Business in the Community is driven in the short term by three-year plans, approved by the board and used as the basis for reporting at the AGM. With so many opportunities for social innovation, Business in the Community is restrained by funding and needs both to conserve its strength and make enlightened choices of investment. Campaigns are increasingly in competition for funding and need to produce convincing business plans as well as demonstrate social benefits.

David Varney is concerned that 20 per cent of FTSE companies are still not in membership. It may be that CSR remains 'off their radar screen', yet in the aftermath of Enron, no company can assume that it has a licence from society to operate at will. Giving to Business in the Community takes two main forms, *financial* through a membership contribution, and *sponsorship*, and through the donation of time and skills of company employees. Interest in voluntary work is burgeoning and this is often the way in which company interest in sponsorship can be aroused.

One of the 'Cares' campaigns has been involved in recruiting support from the local football team (Leeds United) and in using business executives to mentor head teachers. Relationships work in both directions very often, creating two-way learning – insights which have been valuable for society as a whole. Personal relationships often help those involved to 'rewind – fast forward'.

Julia Cleverdon holds monthly executive meetings and team briefings. Every Friday she has an open forum, over tea, so that any concerns may be aired without prejudice. Business in the Community is built on bottom-up support; leadership within teams moves round depending on the issues faced. Business in the Community practises constant communication so that it can be affective and effective. Teams compete with each other for company support so they need to understand other campaigns thoroughly.

Business in the Community does not see itself as a popular brand; it is known to government and business, and many of its key campaigns are household brands for instance. 'Opportunity Now' is famous for the involvement of Lady Howe and Cherie Blair; other campaigns have their own distinguishing features. Loyalty largely lies within the campaigns, driven by the beliefs and agendas of each campaign. Each campaign is led by a leadership team of senior business executives and engages a number of inspirational people committed to it, yet their fervour does not impede the integrating work of Business in the Community. Each knows that Business in the Community is greater than the sum of its parts.

Business in the Community operates in Wales, Northern Ireland and the regions of England. These operations are managed corporately but the mix of campaigns varies according to region. Devolution of power to the regions is restrained by a tendency for individual regions to undertake initiatives which spill into other regions. This is a big and recurrent issue for Business in the Community. Julia Cleverdon spends considerable time 'lubricating' such misunderstandings, with diplomacy rather than direction. Enthusiasm and commitment come 'from the bottom' and passion is crucial for success in social work. Learning to control and channel that passion is a key lesson for young campaigners.

Benchmarking is becoming increasingly important, for example, The Business in the Environment reporting in the *Financial Times*. There is now a Corporate Responsibility Index which has been developed with outside firms. Capacity is needed to audit the processes involved. 122 PLCs – well above the original target of 70 – worked their way through the first Corporate Responsibility Index. This included members and non-members of Business in the Community. The results to date are on the Business in the Community website. The index is based on a framework developed by Business in the Community which tests and rates companies in the areas of strategy, integration, management practice on community environment, marketplace and workplace and performance (in seven important areas, three social and four environmental). Companies are also rated on the level of 'assurance' backing their submission. Ratings are at three levels:

A   Companies measuring and reporting progress
B   Companies moving beyond a basic commitment
C   Companies beginning to make some progress.

The qualities rated are:

i   Corporate strategy and integration combined
ii   Management practice community
iii Management practice environment
iv   Management practice marketplace
v   Management practice workplace.

Performance in their selected impact areas is integrated into the overall management profile. These five ratings become the overall management profile.

Results for FTSE 350 companies are grouped in quintiles to create a league and stimulate competition. Non-FTSE members of Business in the Community are marked separately. For the first index, average overall scores were 67.87 per cent with social impact achieving 64.21 per cent. Highest scoring was in corporate strategy (80.82 per cent) though integration lagged at 61.3 per cent – a revealing gap!

Other indices used by Business in the Community include FTSE 4 Good and the Dow Jones Sustainability Index. Reputation is now a key issue for investors and corporate social responsibility is seen as a talisman for good reputation. There is a growing need to rationalise the different indices for general use; Business in the Community needs to decide which is best for its purpose.

Business in the Community sees its stakeholders as the key business decision makers of major companies who are members, non-member companies (to be persuaded to join), media communities, NGOs, employees, government (national, local) and some trades unions. Strategies to engage stakeholders are well developed but are continually being refined to meet changing needs. Stakeholders are now brought into Business in the Community's strategy process which is directed by the board and focused on the long term. As Chairman, David Varney acts as the key link between the board and the CEO – a major part of his role is helping to make Julia and her management team effective.

Two years ago an exercise was undertaken to evaluate risks in order to meet the requirements of the Turnbull Report. This involved assessing the likelihood and impact of each risk, and allocating responsibility for monitoring and subsequent action. This programme is now subject to regular review by the Finance and Audit Committee of the board.

Business in the Community is a community of activities, and conflict resolution is a key requirement of management and, if necessary, the board. BITC is like an university, full of enthusiasm and ideas, and impatient of funding constraints. The new office is helping to improve communications but there remains a constant potential tension between the regions and the campaigns.

The purpose of Business in the Community can only be served by having clear objectives. Membership is fundamental and the 20 per cent of FTSE companies not yet in membership is a key target. The 1000 companies that would be required to report by law once the new Company Law Review comes into play are also a key target. Another major objective is to increase the number of employee volunteers to support Business in the Community's various campaigns, which, together with conferences and other events, provide vehicles to accomplish the purpose of Business in the Community. Leadership is a key element of Business in the Community's role. It needs to make its activities fully relevant to the requirements of organisations to integrate responsible business practice. Loss of membership is a key measure of failing leadership.

When David Varney was Chief Executive of BG plc he was Chairman of the BG Foundation (latterly the Lattice Foundation) which undertook a number of major community projects, driven by the programme supported by HRH The Prince of Wales 'Seeing is Believing'. One of these was 'Reading Young Offenders', in which young offenders in the Reading area were trained to drive forklift trucks. So far 74 youngsters have completed the course and re-offending has declined to 12 per cent. Another project in Reading focused on exclusion from school and increased attendance rates to 80 per cent. Lloyds TSB sponsored the Portsmouth Area Regeneration Trust (PART) in order to lend money to risk-averse excluded people. After two years it had made 394 loans, with a 'concern' rate of only 6 per cent, and had begun to generate hope and wider interest. It now makes very small loans to ex-offenders and ex-drug addicts in order to support their rehabilitation.

These and other projects are based on business principles, with a wider latitude to experiment than usual, and achieving a slow, but steady, growth in confidence among everyone involved. The board of Business in the Community reviews progress against its objectives regularly. There is no lack of ideas and initiatives but there is a need to make choices and push diversity. Much remains to be done; society is not inclusive and attitudes still need to be changed. Only a small number of members fill in the questionnaires sent to them. A growing number of high-profile figures are active in Business in the Community campaigns, including Alan Leighton, Sir Peter Davis, Derek Higgs, Richard Handover and John Studinski. John Quelch emphasised the reputation of London Business School in order to involve members of his staff. Personalities are important but Business in the Community needs to build its own strong brand, perhaps like Investors in People or 'Children in Need' in a wider context. Its role is to align the energies of enthusiasts to higher purpose. Connecting with problems and aligning support to deal with them is its key challenge. The support of Prince Charles is very motivating, since he is quick to pick up issues and keen to follow progress in dealing with them. David Varney sees Prince Charles some six times per year and can talk to him when necessary.

Business in the Community has long been in the vanguard of the movement for corporate social innovation (CSI) which has now become the cutting edge of the later and wider movement for corporate social responsibility. As a result theory is now wedded to long-standing practice and has provided the impulsion to extend and consolidate that practice. This process is well illustrated in a report by Rachel Jupp for Demos entitled 'Getting Down to Business', which is also a manifesto for a more extensive and embedded approach to responsible business practice, with active government support and the involvement of a greater number of British businesses. The ultimate objective of the process is to create a self-sustaining society, by engaging all sectors in physical, mental and social improvement.

Success in this shared enterprise would have the following features:

- A focus on outcomes (and not just inputs)
- Encouraging wide and active participation
- A focus on the long term (and not just quick wins)
- Wide applicability (to facilitate benchmarking best practice)
- Incorporating and reconciling multiple perspectives
- A focus on knowledge transfer and policy learning.

The future of Business in the Community will be driven partly by measurement. This creates healthy rivalry between organisations and helps to raise involvement and standards. The 'Awards for Excellence' programme is helping to drive this process and to involve companies of all sizes. More needs to be done to build up activity in the regions. Greater involvement by ethnic groups is needed to remove race and religion as causes for exclusion. The 'Cares' programme is likely to continue to grow strongly into the future, leading to government concern about bureaucratising community projects.

Learning from this year's Corporate Responsibility Index has strengthened the need to address workplace issues not yet addressed such as ageing and pensions as a priority issue; it faces the danger of over-expansion and needs now to normalise a process by which it can enable successful campaigns to operate independently under its brand (such as was done with the disability campaign, now 'The Employers' Forum on Disability'). This process of rationalisation is likely to continue, with Business in the Community developing campaigns in key areas and bringing them to viability before passing them to specialist groups to sustain into the future.

Corporate sustainability

ARTICLE 13 – TURNING OBLIGATION INTO OPPORTUNITY

Article 13 was founded in 1998 by Neela Bettridge and Jane Fiona Cumming as a consultancy to advise businesses on how to integrate social responsibility into their way of working. Named after an article on shared understanding in the convention drawn up at the 1992 Earth Summit at Rio, the company's purpose is not to politicise their clients but to reinforce their ability to earn sustainable profits through corporate citizenship. Building a solid reputation among its stakeholders is the way for a company to build profitability.

Article 13 sees corporate governance as the system by which companies are directed and controlled. They identify four strands to corporate governance:

1 Financial accounting
2 The board (including non-executive directors)
3 Stakeholders (including employees)
4 Transparency (how we do business).

Corporate governance is defined as 'the Board's responsibility to owners, shareholders and, increasingly, society'. Corporate governance 'ensures that companies:

- align their policies, systems and activities with their values;
- learn about actual and perceived impacts of their activities;
- implement effective management of risks associated with actual and perceived 'social and environmental' impacts on business process; and
- inform stakeholders to enhance engagement and overall value added through reputational gains'.

1. Financial accounting

The key problems which led the Stock Exchange to commission the Cadbury Inquiry were linked to financial reporting (BCCI, Maxwell, and so on). Financial statements are the basis for communication between a company and its shareholders and other stakeholders. Reliable financial accounting represents the life blood of a business; its failure is usually fatal. It was the series of corporate failures due to false accounting which led to the Sarbanes-Oxley Act in the USA, whereby CEOs and CFOs take personal responsibility for the financial statements of their company.

2. The board

Under company law the board is responsible for the direction of the company. Corporate governance is at the heart of its task and it is accountable to shareholders for effective governance. The board determines the company's strategy which is implemented by the executive directors and their senior staff. Non-executive directors bring external experience and contacts to the board's deliberations and to the monitoring of company performances. They also oversee the balance of power among the members of the board.

3. Stakeholders

Core stakeholders include shareholders, the board, employees, customers, suppliers, distributors and the local community. Other stakeholders are government (national and local), regulators, the wider society and 'the environment'. Media and pressure groups are only stakeholders when they act at the instigation of core or other stakeholders; if acting in pursuit of their own agenda, they are not stakeholders.

4. Transparency

Transparency is a term which subsumes values, behaviours, openness and accountability. It represents 'the way we do business'. Transparency creates trust, enabling a company to operate on principles rather than rules. Principles reflect the values embedded in the company and underlie the policies, systems and activities which drive its business.

Corporate governance

Article 13 sees the 'Board's responsibility to owners, shareholders and, increasingly, society' as a key part of its role in creating wealth. It looks beyond compliance with laws, regulations and codes, to building profitable relationships. Article 13 sees corporate governance as a means to oblige companies to:

- operate in a manner acceptable to society as a whole
- ensure that its actions develop a sustainable future
- create wealth to invest in a better world.

The board should direct the company in a manner befitting its role as a member of society, not as a body with no external responsibilities. Companies depend on their reputation and reputation is earned from society as a whole. Members of the board are trustees of the company and must operate in its interests not their own. Directors should be adequately rewarded but are not on the board to enrich themselves.

Corporate governance needs to focus on the future as well as the present. It needs to ensure that actions taken by the company do not mortgage its future to maximise short term gain. The board needs also to ensure that its decisions do not prejudice the future of other legitimate stakeholders. Innovation should be a key instrument for developing a sustainable future for the company and its stakeholders.

Companies exist to create wealth through enterprise. The wealth created by all enterprise belongs to society as a whole and is allocated through wages, dividends, taxes and other payments. A key feature of corporate governance is to ensure that allocation is both efficient and equitable, while ensuring that the development of the company can be funded and protected from undue risk.

IMPLEMENTING CORPORATE GOVERNANCE

Article 13 operates as a special adviser to organisations on corporate governance and responsibility. It focuses on improving performance in the round, not just profits, and covers economic, social, environmental and ethical performance in its work.

Most organisations find difficulty in taking corporate governance into the daily actions of their staff and of their stakeholders. Too often corporate governance is seen as a compliance issue and as an intrusion on daily work. Article 13 believes that corporate governance is best seen as a means of protecting jobs, through better relationships with customers and other stakeholders, and through encouraging innovation.

Article 13 also works to invigorate organisations through innovation and through 'breaking the cycle'. Many firms see regulation and controls as impediments to their business. Article 13 helps them to turn such 'negatives' into sources of competitive advantage. Corporate social responsibility is a key area of benefit if it is delivered with business-like purpose. Article 13 does not just help its clients to be ethical and socially responsible but to make money through being so.

Implementing corporate governance requires a systematic change in the mindset of all who work in an organisation. This is best achieved by cascading the process of change down through all levels of the structure. Article 13 operates in this manner and has achieved successful change in a wide range of organisations from government, through business to charities.

8 *Risk and Investment*

Risk is the life blood of capitalism but its management is essential for long-term success. The Turnbull Report has made risk management a core element of corporate governance and risks surround us on all sides. Investment management has been drawn into the spotlight of governance by poor performance, partly caused by market risk. Managing risk is now a real issue for the investment industry as it struggles to regain trust.

Control Risks Group

Control Risks Group is a private limited company which has developed out of a consultancy business, specialising in personal security overseas, into a global risk management adviser. The focus of its activities is practical, underpinned by research and innovation, and it works closely with clients to help them develop their solutions to risk issues which they face.

I spoke to John Conyngham, a Director of Control Risks Group, and to Simon Dawson, Associate Director, Corporate Investigations. Both are qualified and experienced lawyers; Conyngham, a barrister, who worked earlier for Kroll, and Dawson, who was a prosecutor. Criminality drives many of the risks faced by clients of Control Risks and deep knowledge of criminal thinking and practice is needed to secure effective protection against such risks.

Money laundering is a major concern worldwide and its control is hampered by increasing globalisation and the Internet. The threat is taken seriously in the USA, leading to the Money Laundering Act, which tightens control both within the USA and extra-territorially. In the Third World, money laundering is often tolerated as a by-product of 'normal trading'; the Asian Development Bank is very concerned about the situation in the Philippines which undermines governmental authority. There is now the beginnings of a sustained crusade against money laundering, supported by major lenders such as the World Bank, so that local accountants and lawyers are finding it increasingly difficult to block investigations. The Royal Bank of Scotland has recently been heavily fined for failing to block a major transaction and all banks are now hypersensitive on this issue. Money laundering is a significant part of the concern of Control Risks and countering it is now a major activity. At present there is no generally accepted legal definition of a 'suspicious transaction' so that it is hard to pinpoint responsibility and avoid the plea of 'I should have realised'.

Security and crisis management are other key areas for Control Risks. Security requires a dedicated manager in every business. Fraud is a difficult process to control; it requires a 'controlled delusion' of all who must be manipulated. Control Risks focuses on fraud awareness training, so that the symptoms can be recognised. In a one-day course clients can learn how to deal with fraud. Training is also given in handling corruption, starting by bringing it out into the open and recognising its different forms. Control Risks' approach is to set aside issues of 'culture' and 'poverty', so that corruption can be addressed as unethical and inefficient. Control Risks has written a manual, *Facing Up to Corruption*, which advises in depth on establishing a clear anti-corruption policy and on how it can be successfully implemented. Precise rules and full operating instructions are developed from a searching dialogue with clients, giving ownership of the issue and the likelihood that the rules will be strictly implemented.

Pressure to deal with corruption is being increased by bodies such as Transparency International. Examples of best practice are now being codified, leading the debate beyond compliance. Companies such as Shell are helping to benchmark best practice and to identify the key indicators needed for control. Control Risks has analysed the processes of corruption and fraud for its clients, both to identify symptoms, for example, failure to report fully or on time, and to recommend actions to counter the risk of default, for example, by segregating duties among different people. It is now possible to evaluate the corporate integrity of a company; this is done by Control Risks in association with Transparency International.

Involving everybody in an organisation is crucial to reducing the risk of fraud or corruption. Investors in People is a very useful process to ensure that this is done comprehensively. Control Risks is often involved in due diligence; due diligence focuses primarily on the people in an organisation. Working with them reveals the tone of the business and helps to guide the processes needed to uncover any weaknesses, many of which may be hiding behind the Data Protection Act.

Control Risks finds that it is easier to gain access to organisations following the Enron and other scandals. Turnbull reporting has opened boardrooms to discussions of risk and has led to the growing trend to appoint risk managers. It is disappointing, however, that only 25 per cent of companies are requiring their reports on risk control to be properly validated.

The Anti-Terrorism Act 2002 has highlighted new risks to companies of all sizes. Corruption helps to feed tension and the extraterritorial provisions of the Act provide new weapons. The Transparency International Indices are also having some effect but corruption can only be attacked effectively by pressure on overseas governments.

Control Risks emphasises the need for clear values and guidelines in client organisations. Given these, the focus is on rigorous processes of staff selection, involving pre-employment screening and clear briefing on stakeholders and business relationships. Procurement needs particular care. Control Risks recommends independent screening of all suppliers and frequent rotation of jobs in the company and its suppliers. Psychometric testing seems to screen out some risks but consistent values are essential to head off aberrance.

Measuring risk is difficult and increasingly complex. The profile of risk in many organisations is so significant that the CFO is challenged to become CRO. Control Risks works with PricewaterhouseCoopers to assess organisations and install fraud prevention mechanisms, including those aimed at securing investment. The process used by Control Risks involves investigation of current procedures and scoring them for effectiveness. Based on this external assessment, a workshop is run which enables staff in the organisation to develop their own self-assessment of fraud risk. This can be benchmarked against the external assessment by Control Risks and differences explored.

Control Risks has pioneered a comprehensive 'Risk Map' which rates risks in all countries and helps organisations to identify and assess specific risks and frame them into a total risk profile for their operations.

One process not used by Control Risks is the 'balanced scorecard'. They remain to be convinced that it works in practice and are concerned about the false sense of precision which it can engender. They do, however, recognise the growing importance of intangibles in controlling risks.

One danger faced by risk managers is fashion. Terrorism has now emerged as more important than fraud or corruption. There is growing concern about the growth of ethnic gangs in the UK. The war in Iraq increased ethnic tension and created new perceived risks to add to those which have yet to be contained. Company boards are now less concerned with Turnbull reporting and risk managers are facing budget constraints as trading revenues fall. Quarterly reporting is now a more pressing issue for most companies than risks for which insurance cover has tripled in cost. There is a danger that risk management may be downgraded in priority until the next crisis occurs. Control Risks believes that external advice and awareness training are crucial to keeping organisations alert to changing patterns of risk. Internal complacency opens the door to risk; eternal vigilance is the price of keeping it closed.

Corporate governance for institutional shareholders
(an interview with Paul Lee of Hermes Investment Management Ltd)

Corporate governance is a recognised issue for quoted companies but has yet to become established in non-quoted companies, or in many of the institutional investors who trade in shares and other investment media. Interest in the issue has been stimulated by regular weekly reviews in the *Financial Times*, entitled 'FT Fund Management', but good practice is limited to a few pioneering institutions at present. One of these is Hermes Investment Management Limited, owned by the BT Pension Scheme, which is one of the largest pension fund managers in the City of London.

Paul Lee emphasised that Hermes maintained a long-term perspective on its investments, typically for 20 years, and sought absolute performance over the long term. This perspective required excellent corporate governance to be successful. Hermes has researched the link between good governance and performance, and a paper by Colin Melvin, Hermes' Director of Corporate Governance, identifies three basic approaches to researching this link:

- Opinion-based research
- Governance ranking
- Focus listing.

Opinion-based research by McKinsey ('Global Investor Opinion survey') found that 80 per cent of respondents would pay a premium for well-governed companies. This premium varied from 11 per cent for Canadian companies to some 40 per cent in poorly regulated countries. A survey of *Fortune* magazine's 'most admired firms' by Antunovich et al found that the 'most admired' firms had an average financial return of 125 per cent whereas the 'least admired' averaged 80 per cent. *Business Week* found in 1997 and 2000 that companies with the highest governance rankings achieved the highest financial returns.

The largest ranking study was that of Gompers et al in 2001. This comprised 1500 US companies and showed that a fund taking long positions on companies in the top decile of governance ranking, and short positions on companies in the bottom decile, would have out-performed the market by 8.5 per cent throughout the 1990s. Gompers' findings have been confirmed by other studies in Europe. A study by the Institute of Business Ethics in 2002 found that companies with codes of ethics outperformed those who did not report having such codes.

Focus lists are issued to publicise corporate governance weaknesses of individual companies with a view to forcing remedial action. Research on the results of such lists from CALPERS and others has shown that they can improve performance both in corporate governance and profitability. The latest evidence of the 'CALPERS effect' (1997) shows that listed companies outperformed the average by 23 per cent in five years after listing, compared with an 89 per cent under-performance in the previous five years. Success with the 'CALPERS effect' has not been general; a recent study by Caton et al suggested that this may be due to failure to distinguish between companies with potential to improve and others. The study found that companies with a Tobin's Q greater than one showed a 7 per cent out-performance 90 days after their listing was announced. This underlines the importance of active ownership in improving company performance (supported by the evidence of Hermes' first Focus Fund, established in October 1998, with BT Pension Fund as an initial investor which by 30 June 2003 had achieved a 28.6 per cent return – 33.2 per cent above the FTSE All-share total return index). In the words of Colin Melvin, 'Companies with active, interested and involved shareholders will tend to outperform'. Hermes has codified what companies and active shareholders should expect from each other in 'The Hermes Principles'. These are:

COMMUNICATION

Principle 1: 'Companies should seek an honest, open and ongoing dialogue with shareholders. They should clearly communicate the plans they are pursuing and the likely financial and wider consequences of those plans. Ideally goals, plans and progress should be discussed in the annual report and accounts.'

FINANCIAL

Principle 2: 'Companies should have appropriate measures and systems in place to ensure that they know which activities and competencies contribute most to maximising shareholder value.'

Principle 3: 'Companies should ensure all investment plans have been honestly and critically tested in terms of their ability to deliver long-term shareholder value.'

Principle 4: 'Companies should allocate capital for investment by seeking fully and creatively to exploit opportunities for growth within their core businesses rather than seeking unrelated diversification. This is particularly true when considering acquisitive growth.'

Principle 5: 'Companies should have performance evaluation and incentive systems designed cost-effectively to incentivise managers to deliver long-term shareholder value.'

Principle 6: 'Companies should have an efficient capital structure which will minimise the long-term cost of capital.'

STRATEGIC

Principle 7: 'Companies should have and continue to develop coherent strategies for each business unit. These should ideally be expressed in terms of market prospects and of the competitive advantage the business has in exploiting these prospects. The company should understand the factors which drive market growth, and the particular strengths which underpin its competitive position.'

Principle 8: 'Companies should be able to explain why they are the "best parent" of the businesses they run. Where they are not best parent they should be developing plans to resolve the issue.'

SOCIAL, ETHICAL AND ENVIRONMENTAL

Principle 9: 'Companies should manage effectively relationships with their employees, suppliers and customers and with others who have a legitimate interest in the company's activities. Companies should behave ethically and have regard for the environment and society as a whole.'

Principle 10: 'Companies should support voluntary and statutory measures which minimise the externalisation of costs to the detriment of society at large.'

Hermes' emphasis on 'shareholder value' is wider than the interests of a pure trader. Its approach to investment is closer to that of an owner – looking to the long term and concerned to create a sustainable business. The concept of 'parenthood' in Principle 8 underlines the responsible and committed approach of Hermes to its investments.

The thoughtful and balanced approach of Hermes is well attuned to the Combined Code and the Higgs Code. This is not surprising since Hermes helped to shape both Codes and is fully supportive of them. Hermes shares the same concern as Higgs to strengthen company boards through the recruitment of independent directors. The performance of the boards of companies in which Hermes invests is monitored closely and Hermes does not hesitate to intervene where necessary. It has even taken strong action where necessary; for example, the chief executive's remuneration at GlaxoSmithKline. Most of Hermes' intervention is private but it votes at all AGMs where possible and votes against resolutions in roughly 3 per cent of cases. Most challenges take place before the resolutions are formulated; here too Hermes is frequently successful. Most of the negative votes are against the election of individual directors (two thirds) or against pay awards (one third). Hermes rarely votes against the adoption of the accounts, preferring to focus on supporting the quality of audit committees. Directors' pay has been a long-running issue, with concerns accelerating since the late 1990s. Some companies seem slow to change their policies on pay. Hermes engages actively with companies which have significant negative votes on pay resolutions.

Paul Lee sees real change achievable only where there is a new pattern of non-executive directors. Change is beginning in age patterns (National Express now has a 38-year-old chairman) and more women are now being appointed. There is a growing interest in treating directorship as a profession, expecting individuals to be qualified to work on a company board and to show independence of mind. Hermes believes in director training, for example, Cranfield courses and has endorsed (after careful assessment) the IoD concept of 'Chartered

Director'. Another improvement being sought is to find non-executive directors with wider experience, not just executive directors from another company but with experience in other parts of society. Hermes believes that it is the personal qualities of a director which are paramount – their ability to reason and make judgements, to research for evidence and to make a sound case. Above all non-executives must be experienced and principled; there are now more who are well off and unwilling to be demoted. They must be willing to challenge and to keep pursuing difficult issues, and they must not be shy of asking simple questions – which are often the hardest to answer. Most of the skills needed can be found today in the private equity sector, among successful entrepreneurs who are willing to work with others. Truly independent directors are those who are keen to work as a team but who are willing to challenge poor teamwork, bad judgement or abuse of power. Long tenure blunts the sharpness of such directors so that truly independent directors are likely to be nomadic.

Hermes and its owner have investments in over 3500 companies worldwide. It cannot give each comprehensive attention so it engages with governments and regulators to ensure the most favourable regulatory framework for minority shareholders, and seeks to vote in all cases where this is not impractical and makes its staff available for consultation by investee companies when requested. In a small number of cases closer engagement is required. In the UK, Hermes invests in some 800 companies; of these 100 are given 'Tier 2' treatment and 10 to 12 'Tier 1' treatment. Additionally there are two Focus Funds in the UK which have 30 companies receiving close attention. Tier 2 engagements discuss concerns about the 'structural' governance of investee companies: principally, board composition, succession planning and pay. Tier 1 engagements also focus discussion on strategic concerns and capital structure issues. Focus Fund engagements are like Tier 1 engagements except that the fund buys an additional stake in the investee company so that clients can enjoy the financial upside which engagement helps create. This level of coverage means that over four to five years, Hermes will have engaged to one extent or another with around 50% of the UK market. These techniques are replicated in other world markets in which Hermes invests, although resource constraints limit the scale of involvements: Hermes engages with perhaps 5 per cent of its clients' holdings in continental Europe, the USA and Japan. In addition, there are occasional engagements elsewhere in the world.

Paul Lee talked about co-operation between institutional investors in order to improve corporate governance. Hermes has had a long relationship with CALPERS which helps to develop thinking and share experience. To work with other investors Hermes was a founder member of the Corporate Governance Forum, which now has about a dozen members and which helps to share information on developments in the market place. The forum facilitates frank and confidential discussion of issues so that, although members vote independently, they are aware of the feelings of fellow members. It tends to be the case that companies react better to separate approaches rather than delegations. The forum often shares perspectives on key issues and has shared concerns on particular companies.

Hermes is very concerned at recent trends in directors' remuneration. The escalation of pay has been driven by US companies and has not yet been bridled. The expensing of options may help to curb some excess since options have been seen as 'costless'. Delays in garnering support for the Financial Accounting Standards Board (FASB) have not helped but CALPERS has been very active in driving for change. CALPERS is also pushing for the use of performance hurdles in the US. Europe has better performance criteria, but these often are too low.

Hermes believes in shareholder value (Principle 9). It seeks to act as an 'enlightened shareholder' to build long-term value, recognising that such value will only be created and sustained by maintaining positive relations with employees, customers, suppliers and society as a whole. The Operating and Financial Report (OFR) report built into the Companies Bill will help to clarify true performance and sustainability, if companies take the opportunity to be more transparent about the underlying drivers of their business. For example, at the moment, too much disclosure on CSR issues is a PR exercise rather than a discussion of how stakeholder relationships are maintained and enhanced in the interests of building profits, and of how the company manages the risks it faces to ensure that shareholder value is not destroyed.

Paul Lee welcomed the Statement of Principles of the Institutional Shareholders' Committee. This was first promulgated in 1991 but now reflects the requirements of the Combined Code, as modified to include the Higgs Report. In June 2003 a 'Survey of Fund Managers' Engagement with Companies' was proposed by the Investment Management Association. This was the first review of actual practice by fund managers and shows some progress towards more systematic and open engagement by fund managers. Out of 33 fund managers surveyed, 28 had clear policies on engagement, of which half were public documents. The other five fund managers had policies in draft. It emerged that many fund managers retained corporate governance specialists but integrated company engagement into the investment process. This suggests that corporate governance is still not integrated into the investment policy in many cases. One positive sign was that the majority of fund managers surveyed had a policy to vote all their UK shares; they also avoided any automatic support for the board of companies in which they invested. Most fund managers believed, however, that a constructive dialogue with company managers was the best approach to achieving change. Voting against the board was a last resort in most cases. Of the 33 fund managers surveyed, 29 reported to their clients quarterly, one monthly and another at client request. These reports covered voting activity (although only four gave details of the resolutions on which they voted).

The survey was repeated in June 2004 and it showed slow overall improvements in performance. It is to be hoped that corporate governance issues (and even CSR matters) will have moved into the core investment process of a greater number of fund managers. The evidence for the link between good governance and profitability is now too significant to ignore. Action to enforce better governance cannot come too soon.

These case studies will hopefully illustrate the principles of corporate governance as they are interpreted and practised by specific groups of organisation. In most cases the focus is on commercial companies but the majority of these cases can be adapted to the voluntary sector, particularly where voluntary organisations are becoming more commercial and accountable. Much of the content of the case studies is also applicable in the public sector, although improvements in the public sector will probably be needed less in terms of structure and process but more in the human aspects of governance.

9 The Future of Corporate Governance

From time to time Shell produces a set of global scenarios which it uses for internal planning and shares with the wider world. Shell pioneered the use of scenario planning in the business world and has helped make it one of the most flexible and valuable business tools of all time.

In 2002 Shell published a new set of global scenarios, 'People and Connections', which explore alternative paths into the future and the different worlds which emerge in 20 years' time. These scenarios may be found at www.shell.com/scenarios but it may be useful to explore their effects on the future of corporate governance.

The first scenario in 'People and Connections' is entitled 'Business Class'. It describes a world which is run like a business, with a focus on efficiency and individual freedom of choice. Globalisation has brought increasing benefits to both rich and poor societies, but growing inequality. This inequality is tolerable as long as individuals see opportunities to improve their lives and have the liberty to pursue their personal dreams. The process of globalisation is driven by highly inter-connected global elites worldwide, whose power is based on wealth and whose principles of deregulation and choice animate all global economic institutions (World Bank, IMF, WTO). The USA remains the sole dominant superpower in this scenario and the 'Washington Consensus' is the road map for global growth. This scenario foresees the emergence of new sources of power, for example, cities which diminish the power of national governments to create a 'new medievalism' (perhaps a new Hanseatic League?). Businesses employ cutting-edge strategies to cope with volatility and greater competition. Gas is the 'great game' in energy, because consumers believe it to be healthy and environmentally friendly, and businesses want it as a new source of wealth and need it for fuel cell market development. This is a scenario for convergence which shifts power from elected bodies to a globally inter-connected elite, whose growing prosperity depends on sharing some of the wealth from globalisation with the consumers who make it possible.

The second scenario is entitled 'Prism'. It questions the 'monochromatic' world of global integration. It is based on the idea that it is the interplay of the differences in humanity which shape the future rather than what we have in common. Just as a prism breaks a single beam of light into multiple bands of different colours, human experience breaks one species into multiple groups with divergent interests and values. 'Prism' is about a future based on multiple alternatives, so that progress and 'Westernisation' are not concomitant, and there are multiple roads towards a better future. 'Prism' has its own interconnected circles of global elites, which are concerned about interests which overlap and which are sustainable. Pressures of modernisation continue in 'Prism' but people seek multiple modernities which are in harmony with their roots and values, rather than the pursuit of pure efficiency. This process creates diverse environments and multiple outcomes. The key requirement for business is to relate to different stakeholders with varying values, so that the ability to gain access to multiple groups and win their trust is essential. Oil remains the dominant global fuel for another two decades but oil companies need to build a platform for transition to a post oil world.

Prism is a scenario for divergence which empowers diverse groups and makes 'Westernisation' one of a number of models of modernity, not the sole passport to progress. Power is likely to be more diffuse in this scenario so that government at all levels will be weaker and special interest groups stronger. Co-operation between disparate groups will be essential to maintain the fabric of society.

Broad characteristics of governance under 'Business Class' and 'Prism' scenarios

Given the different nature of each scenario, its influence on the main issues in corporate governance is likely to diverge. The following schedule indicates the broad characteristics of governance issues under each scenario:

	Business Class	*Prism*
Tone of governance	Deregulated	Regulated
Means of governance	Codes	Laws
Power	Controlled delegation	Diffused
Leadership	Grouped	Distributed
Stakeholders	Managed	Embraced
Ethics	Managed	Embraced
Trust	Conditional	Embraced
Openness	Conditional	Embraced
Integrity	Conditional	Isolated
Accountability	As needed	Diffused
Collaboration	Managed	Case by case
Shareholders	More assertive but no nineteenth-century power	Lose out to stakeholders
Communications	Greater use of Internet	Reliant on Internet
Human relations	Formal, only core employed	Informal, fragmented
Government	Beholden to business	Fragmented

The scenarios and their possible impact on corporate governance

Corporate governance in the 'Business Class' scenario will probably be influenced by some of the following factors:

• Greater corporate visibility may increase pressures for openness and accountability.

- Corporate governance may need to be formalised to protect stakeholders from elites' economic power.
- Business becomes more influential and the power of politicians/government weakens.
- Increasing international competition will put a premium on efficiency (risk of cartels).
- Business will press for deregulation in order to improve efficiency and lower costs.
- The elites will support measures to protect themselves from crime and terrorism.
- The Internet will be used to improve efficiency primarily.
- Innovation will be driven by efficiency concerns primarily (need to encourage/protect entrepreneurs).
- The elites will need to ensure 'trickledown' of benefits to protect them from resentment.
- Media will have a key role to protect the underprivileged from exploitation, and to prevent the formation of cartels.

What may be the characteristics of a 'Business Class' scenario in 2020 in the field of corporate governance? Such characteristics may include:

- Greater visibility of companies (due to media). Will this increase openness and accountability?
- If there is greater openness and accountability, comparison is facilitated.
- Formalised governance to protect stakeholders from the power of the elites.
- Individual aspirations may be curtailed by the power of the elites.
- Efficiency may conflict with personal freedom.
- Efficiency may be achieved by constraining competition.
- Deregulation should facilitate efficiency, but will accountability be weakened?
- Politicians are less powerful (accountable?) as business drives the system.
- Crime may be more contained where it threatens the interests of the elites.
- Innovation may be driven by efficiency rather than creativity.
- The Internet may be used for efficiency rather than freedom.
- Unless there is 'trickledown' to the disadvantaged this scenario may build resentment.
- The media may have a role to protect the disadvantaged and stabilise the scenario.

'Prism' may have the following consequences for corporate governance:

- Visibility may be low, due to fragmentation (media attention will be dispersed).
- Poorer visibility may weaken openness and accountability. It may be harder to contain corruption.
- Poorer visibility may make it more difficult to compare businesses (and weaken competition).
- Special interest groups will have strong internal relationships; between them relationships may be volatile.
- It may be harder to contain crime in this scenario (poor visibility, weak relationships).
- Innovation is likely to be lively, but chaotic.
- Groups may use contracts/law to define their relationships. Enforcement may be harder as some nations have weaker institutions.
- Groups may be transnational and linked by shared interest (using the Internet) rather than national.
- Regulation is likely to be more necessary (but enforcement more difficult).

- Internet usage will integrate groups worldwide. To what external body can they be accountable?
- Tribalism is likely to be reinforced in this scenario and civil society weakened.

What actions are needed to shape corporate governance to be effective in 2020?

In both 'Business Class' and 'Prism' there are significant potential challenges to effective corporate governance. 'Business Class' reflects a world in which global business drives the economy and influences the working of society. Greater visibility of business activities should favour deregulation, unless the 'elites' become 'oligarchs' and manage to obscure their operations. The Russian government purge of 'oligarchs' may be difficult to achieve on the global scale of 'Business Class'. In 'Business Class' the USA is expected to strengthen as a role model and English may retain its dominance as a language. While old models of privilege (for example, royalty) may wither, it is likely that behind a façade of republicanism the 'elites' will create new dynasties and hierarchies in order to sustain and perpetuate themselves. As China, India and other new lead players emerge on to the world stage, the hegemony of the USA and the influence of Europe may be diluted and modified. 'Business Class' does not assume the continuing dominance of 'the Western world', only the globalisation of business interests. If business interests become powerful enough to contain competition and resurrect the cartels of the past it is possible that corporate governance may move into decline.

In the case of 'Prism' a world of multiple alternatives will encourage varying models of corporate governance and make the setting of benchmarks more difficult. The dispersion of media attention will hamper attempts to encourage best practice. Lack of visibility may encourage the proliferation of 'rogue operators' in the style of Barlow Clowes, leading to repeated scandals such as those which gave impetus to the search for improved corporate governance in the 1980s and the tightening of regulation to achieve it. The tensions between different clans and interest groups in 'Prism' may lead to the fragmentation of several 'nation states' (as with Czechoslovakia). While the need for greater regulation may become apparent, the ability of governments to impose and police it may weaken. A strong legal system is essential in the 'Prism' scenario to enable groups to contract and to protect their property; this may underpin governments which would otherwise be undermined by conflicting special interests. 'Prism' will offer multiple and complex challenges to effective governance throughout society, not only in the corporate sector.

The actions needed to shape corporate governance to be effective in 2020 and beyond are both generic and specific to the needs of each scenario. Generic actions would seem to include the following:

- Encouraging an independent and critical press and other media. (This requires distributed ownership, no government involvement and responsible justice from the courts.)
- Making challenge respectable in public life (to defeat cronyism and apathy).
- Raising the hurdles of accountability (set higher standards and enforce them). (Need to make reporting more strategic. Quarterly reporting should be abolished.)
- Taking further action against market manipulation and insider dealing.

- Having independent regulation of auditors, higher professional standards and abolishing the cartel. (Auditors should only audit; all other advice may conflict with the audit. Clients should have a bigger choice of auditor, break up big firms and operate internationally by association. The size of audit fees should be explained and challenged, not seen as a 'macho' symbol.)
- Making directorship a profession, independent of management. Developing professional non-executive directors equipped to challenge their executive colleagues. Directors should be licensed and regulated by a professional body.
- External appraisal of board effectiveness should be required for all listed companies (as proposed by the Higgs Report).
- The market for executive directors should be opened to competition. They should be paid as hired hands, not as shareholders. Strategy should be set by the board and delivered by the executive directors.
- Companies should be required to make the information they give relevant to all stakeholders not just to stock analysts, as at present.

'BUSINESS CLASS'

In this scenario there will be a number of specific actions needed to make corporate governance effective. They may include:

- Increasing social and environmental accountability.
- Clarifying the distinction between ownership of the company and the custodial role of directors. (The 'elites' may have both roles but must keep them distinct.)
- Increasing external monitoring of company operations, for example, to avoid corruption. (This will require a stronger internal audit and Audit Committee, supported by consultants answerable only to the Audit Committee.)
- A majority of non-executive directors should be independent of the 'elites'.
- Directors should be chosen on merit from all sectors of global society (women, different social and ethnic groups, and so on).

'PRISM'

In this scenario there will also be a number of specific actions needed to make corporate governance effective. These may include:

- Establishing an agreed code of values for directing the company (to avoid the confusion of multiple choice).
- Establishing an agreed mission for the company and seeing it as a benchmark for all decisions (to avoid policy drift).
- Directing the company on a sustainable basis and winning commitment from stakeholders to support sustainable policies and strategies.
- Developing a board of directors with the skills needed to focus on achieving consistent results while coping with multiple stakeholders (ability to handle conflict, ambiguity and maintain consistency).
- Increasing the visibility of the company and communicating fully with stakeholders.
- Building and sustaining loyalty between the company and its stakeholders, so that both deliver on their mutual commitments.

Present trends in corporate governance and the impact of the scenarios on them

It is possible to identify certain trends in corporate governance and it is useful to test them against the two scenarios:

1 *Greater enforcement of rules/codes in the USA, for example Sarbanes-Oxley, Eliot Spitzer, and so on*
   There is already growing resistance from business to this trend. Under 'Business Class' it may weaken further; under 'Prism' it may dissipate its energies. Sean Harrigan has already been dismissed from CALPERS for being over active as a shareholder.

2 *Compliance in Europe is more procedural (and subject to tacit evasion)*
   Unless and until there are further scandals, policing is not likely to be severe. There is a stand-off between regulators and companies, though Brussels may increase pressure. Under 'Business Class' the balance may swing away from regulators to business, unless there are new scandals of some magnitude. Under 'Prism' there may be a gradual move to substitute laws for codes.

3 *Refining the audit process*
   Most countries are moving towards the rotation of auditors (just audit partners so far) and some are barring auditors from other work for the same client. Now that there are only four global firms of auditors and each is faced with mounting litigation risks, corporate governance may face a crisis of audit competence, unless smaller firms continue to form global partnerships. MORI has revealed a significant lack of public trust in the audit of companies, partly due to poor communication in accessible language (see 'Focus on the Future of Corporate Governance', MORI, June 2003). Under 'Business Class' global firms will be subject to increased visibility, making the quality of their audit crucial. Poor auditing will carry severe penalties from clients and other stakeholders. If reforms under generic actions on p. 130 fail, might governments (if they remain capable of doing so) be forced to be auditors of last resort? Under 'Prism' auditing may have less scrutiny but poor auditors will be subject to litigation (and more exposed to the greater risks inherent in this scenario of crime and corruption).

4 *Non-executive directors*
   The Higgs Report has reinforced pressure to appoint better non-executive directors (NEDs) and to rebalance the pattern of power on boards. There remains considerable resistance to adopting Higgs' recommendations, particularly from executive directors, and there is a growing shortage of competent and willing NEDs. Fees have doubled in many cases in order to find them. MORI finds that 64 per cent of NEDs have had no training from their company. It is to be hoped that independent chairpeople and a majority of NEDs will make boards more demanding and effective, and enable strategy to be debated more effectively among all directors, rather than imposed by the CEO. Holding the executive directors to account will be a crucial new challenge for NEDs. Under 'Business Class' NEDs may face the problem of 'elite' directors acting as proprietors, and unless independent directors are a majority, there may be constant manoeuvring between the 'elites' and each new set of NEDs appointed. Under 'Prism' there may be pressure to appoint stakeholder

representatives as directors; this should be strongly resisted if the company is to maintain a consistent strategic direction.

5 *Executive directors' remuneration*
The example of the demands of sports and film stars may have helped to inflate executive directors' pay which in many cases is 100 times that of average employees and often much more. Boards have failed to set and enforce performance standards so that rewards are often unmerited and sanctions non-punitive. MORI finds that 78 per cent of respondents feel that executive directors are overpaid. Despite frequent challenges from media, abuse continues and a new wave of NEDs has a major problem to solve. Under 'Business Class' controlling the 'elites' will present a problem and corporations will escalate pay to higher levels. It may be necessary to stop 'elites' building a power base in the company they direct through acquiring shares. Directors are servants not masters. The risk that American excesses will become a global norm is real and must be countered. Under 'Prism' lack of visibility may tempt directors to indulge themselves unless NEDs are truly independent. The complex world of 'Prism' also facilitates corruption and fraud.

6 *Corporate social responsibility*
Following Shell's mishaps in Nigeria and with Brent Spar there has developed a move by companies with high public exposure to embrace corporate social responsibility (CSR). This started with the oil and other 'problematic' businesses, but has now become a mainstream activity. Focus on reputational risk since Enron and other scandals has also driven this movement. There is some reaction to this trend (a feeling that Shell 'took its eye off the ball' when it miscalculated its reserves, for instance). Nevertheless stakeholder concern seems to have made CSR irreversible. Under 'Business Class' CSR is likely to be pursued as a public relations exercise, rather than from deeper conviction. As with Nike it carries the danger of seeming insincere if reality does not match the image. Under 'Prism' CSR may threaten to become a growing distraction from the priorities of the business.

7 *Convergence of corporate governance between countries and between the public, private and voluntary sectors*
Corporate governance, as a movement, started in the UK and has gradually spread to Organisation for Economic Co-operation and Development (OECD) countries and beyond. Most have followed the voluntary code approach of the UK and involve minimal regulation. Sarbanes-Oxley has brought legislation into play and it may be that the voluntary approach will not survive continuing disappointments in performance. In parallel with the Cadbury Code, the UK public sector developed the Nolan Inquiry which was driven by principles rather than rules. Nolan seems to have been more successful, in a quieter way than Cadbury, and the 'principles' approach offers greater flexibility for those trusted to use it. One potential trend is to integrate Nolan and Cadbury (as the public and private sectors move towards convergence). Alternatively the Cadbury model may be recast in a legal form and be attached to the Companies Act. Under 'Business Class' it is likely that deregulation will be in favour, so that the Cadbury/Hampel model may continue. Any major problems will be open to litigation under the Companies Act or other relevant law. Under 'Prism' the lack of transparency caused by complexity will tempt businesses to seek clarity through the law, so that corporate governance may be subject to statute.

8 *Shareholder activism*

Much of the mischief in the corporate sector has been encouraged in the past by lack of shareholder involvement in their investments. Shareholders now have access to more information than ever before but fund managers have until recently been reluctant to challenge incumbent management. The example of CALPERS in the USA and the patient prodding of Pensions and Investment Research Consultants (PIRC) in the UK are now beginning to change this attitude of misguided loyalty (or inertia?). Fund managers, such as Hermes (see Chapter 8), are increasingly active in managing their portfolio and influencing policy in the companies in which they invest. Some, such as Knight Vinke, are active in reconstructing major groups in order both to release value and to stimulate better governance. Knight Vinke prompted the reconstruction of Shell and is now targeting Suez. It is to be hoped that institutional shareholders will lend weight to private shareholders in demanding more effective governance from the companies in which they invest. This complex activity is now becoming integrated through the International Corporate Governance Network, led by Anne Simpson (formerly of PIRC) and backed by the world's largest investment funds. Under 'Business Class' it is likely that this process will tend to revert to discreet 'clubbiness' which should be challenged by media and all stakeholders. Under 'Prism' institutional investors will need to be more active in order to protect the board from being distracted from the growth of the company by the claims of multiple lobbies.

Integrating corporate governance into strategy

Many critics of corporate governance see it as a distraction from the pursuit of the long-term interests of the company. The present fashion for CSR has reinforced the concerns of such critics, some of whom see corporate governance becoming the end rather than the means of achieving a higher purpose. To date much of the debate about corporate governance has focused on structure and process, largely to redress earlier weaknesses, but the debate now needs to move on to a strategic plane.

Certain strategic issues have been brought out in the debate so far. The role of the board in developing strategy has been confirmed and the Turnbull Report has increased concern about managing risk. This concern is, however, focused currently on operational and asset risks and lacks a real strategic dimension. The interest in reputational risk was stimulated by external events, for example, Enron, and has been echoed by Shell's mismanagement of its reporting of reserves. More work needs to be done to develop a strategic dimension to risk management, largely by exploring the changing nature of risk into the future and descrying new risks over the horizon. St Andrews Management Institute (through its affiliate SAMI Consulting) is using scenario planning to develop risk management strategies, particularly in financial services.

The next major strategic issue in corporate governance is the Operating and Financial Report (OFR) which will be required under the proposed new Companies Act. The purpose of the OFR is stated to be 'to provide a discussion and analysis of the performance of the business and the main trends and factors underlying the results and financial position and likely to affect performance in the future, so as to enable users to assess the strategies adopted by the business and the potential for successfully achieving them' (Company Law Review Document, July 2001). The following topics need to be addressed in the OFR:

- The company's business and business objectives, strategy and principal drivers of performance.
- A fair review of the development of the company's business over the year and position at the end of it, including material post year-end events, operating performance and material change.
- The dynamics of the business, that is, known events, trends, uncertainties and the factors which may substantially affect future performance, including investment programmes (Company Law Review). Companies are encouraged to add any other information specific to the company and its markets which makes the review more pertinent. Companies quoted on the Stock Exchange are also required to address the issue of risk in order to meet the requirements of the Turnbull Report.

Great emphasis is laid on the avoidance of box ticking, so that the OFR is fixed in form but fluid in content. Imaginative preparation of the OFR will allow companies to demonstrate a strategic understanding of their business and its key drivers as well as an appraisal of the context in which it will need to operate into the future. The OFR offers companies the opportunity to compete for investor attention not merely in figures of past performance but in demonstrating their sustainability. To do so companies will need to enhance their strategic thinking and build a reputation for anticipating future opportunities and threats with consistency and delivering a reliable performance.

How can companies enhance their strategic thinking? One major step forward is to involve a wider circle of stakeholders and external experts in the process of strategic analysis, so that the process is more challenging, fewer key issues are missed or misunderstood and a wider range of options for strategy emerges. Wider involvement creates wider ownership and a better understanding of what each stakeholder can contribute to and expect from the growth of the business. In the past, strategy has been developed behind closed doors to preserve confidentiality. Using the best principles of corporate governance the development of strategic options can be shared with stakeholders, leaving the final choice of strategies and investment to support them to the board.

In such a two-stage approach to strategy the second stage also requires a new approach. At present many boards allow the CEO to develop a strategic plan which they endorse. Many boards have 'away days' in which the strategic situation of the business is discussed and strategies debated. Too often it is the CEO who runs these events and may be tempted to 'stage manage' them. In a situation where Higgs is requiring a board with a majority of NEDs and an independent chairperson, it makes more sense to have a process open to wider contribution. If NEDs control the Audit Committee in order to prevent misfeasance and the Remuneration Committee to demonstrate impartiality, and now have greater influence in Nomination Committees, does the key area of strategy not need a more open approach? In my book, *Strategic Leadership*, I recommend the creation of a Strategy Committee, comprising NEDs and the company secretary, to take expert evidence from the corporate planner and from managers involved in strategic planning, to ensure that the detailed workings of the planning system are satisfactory. In the light of the failure of so many companies to deliver their strategic plans, it must be recognised that implementation is an area for concern. By involving a wider range of stakeholders in shaping strategic options, and having plans developed by the whole board, implementation should improve. In order for NEDs to contribute more effectively to the process, the creation of a Strategy Committee, in which novel strategies can be developed 'offline' and the working of the planning system 'audited' independently, may have found its moment. The learning from the Strategy Committee will reinforce the confidence of NEDs in debating strategy with their executive colleagues and ensure that it is the board as an entity which shapes the strategic plan. It is then the role of the executive directors to oversee and ensure its implementation.

How corporate governance may evolve

Corporate governance emerged as an issue following a series of frauds which were damaging confidence in the City in the late 1980s. Its initial focus was on financial reporting but it developed a detailed set of standards (the 'Cadbury Code') for the board to meet in order to rebuild confidence among the investment community. Sir Adrian Cadbury always intended the scope of corporate governance to cover all aspects of company direction, both internal and external, and the wider spectrum was addressed through the 'Tomorrow's Company' Report of 1995 and the subsequent movement it engendered. This movement emphasises the need for 'inclusiveness' in managing companies and recognises a range of stakeholders whose involvement is essential for sustainable success. Among new stakeholders are the out-sourced operations which many companies seek to forget but which remain essential for their future success. The increasing trend to share supply chains in global markets creates another new stakeholder relationship for those involved. This impetus for widening the scope of corporate governance has also been reinforced by the development of corporate social responsibility (CSR) and concern for the environment.

Corporate governance may evolve towards a focus on the relationship between shareholders and the board of directors. A reaction against 'stakeholderism' is evident in Elaine Sternberg's book *Corporate Governance: Accountability in the Market Place* (IEA, 1998, 2004), and a new book by John Carver, the US guru, and Caroline Oliver, *Corporate Boards that Create Value* (Jossey-Bass, 2004) puts the total focus of corporate governance on the board and its relationship with shareholders. Carver believes that boards should direct management and not share power with managers. Corporate governance is seen as the instrument for boards to transmit the will of owners into action. The book develops and promotes a Policy Governance Model which empowers the board as a whole and directs management to meet the wishes of owners.

Deepening the effect of corporate governance

Progress in widening the scope of corporate governance leaves much to be done in deepening it. Too many companies' boards treat corporate governance as an imposition, like regulation, rather than a way of managing to be used to strengthen their business. Few companies have succeeded in taking corporate governance, and the shared values which animate it, right down through their organisation. BP seems to have made more progress than most but the task remains substantially incomplete. How may success in integrating corporate governance be recognised and measured? One promising indicator is the rating of companies as being 'good to work for', undertaken by *Fortune* ('Great Companies to Work For', 2 February 2004). Employees seem to like a distinctive culture and a clear social mission. Such companies find it easier to recruit and retain productive employees, who speak well of their company to outsiders and help to build a strong image in the market place. More work needs to be done to extend such appraisals on an objective and comparable basis to other stakeholders; most customer surveys are limited in scope and ephemeral. It is work of this nature which may help to avoid tipping the balance from light regulation towards a more legalistic regime.

As corporate governance begins to have more impact on the running of companies (the ABI Report for 2004 shows 70 per cent of FTSE 100 companies meeting the terms of the Combined Code), there seems to be the beginnings of a reaction from some quarters. This is more obvious in the USA where Sarbanes-Oxley is biting hard. In the UK remuneration is the centre of resistance, although independent directors in the Higgs mould may begin to make for change. Where companies are not in the limelight the spread of good practice is slower and more uneven. On both sides of the Atlantic, executive remuneration will continue to be a battlefield; in Europe the disclosure of remuneration is still easy to avoid in many countries. Where the remuneration of CEOs is disclosed, as in the USA, it is revealed to be often 500 times that of an average employee! Surely this is yet another unsustainable bubble!

The implementation of the Operating and Financial Report (OFR) should lead to greater accountability from the board and will hopefully act as a spur to improving strategic performance. If the OFR helps to rebalance the appraisal of companies away from the short term towards building a sustainable future it will have made a major contribution to effective corporate governance.

In a world where principles are having to be relearned, corporate governance will continue to rely on alert regulation. The history of regulation in the UK and elsewhere is full of examples of belated 'stable door shutting', most recently in insurance misselling. A new threat is emerging in the areas of life assurance consolidation where closed funds are 'run off' to extinction. There is a danger that asset strippers may move in to plunder these funds; the latest move involves the purchase by Hugh Osmond of funds demerged from AMP and the risk that revenue may be diverted from pension holders to shareholders. This is part of a discernible trend and serves notice that corporate governance is constantly imperilled.

It seems unlikely that corporate governance will ever change human nature. Greed and fear are the basic motivators of humankind since the time of Adam and civilisation is only skin deep, as Pol Pot's 'killing fields' and other horrors constantly remind us. Corporate governance is part of a process of building a better world, based on shared values, which can produce growing wealth and new opportunity for sharing it more widely. At present corporate governance has not even won full acceptance in the boardroom and has touched few of the employees and other stakeholders who are needed to help to embed it in the daily routine of business. Like a new pair of shoes it is shiny but pinches uncomfortably. It will have more impact when it is worn unconsciously, is accepted as normal and operates unseen.

3 *Appendices*

A *BusinessTown.com*

Profile of an entrepreneur

DO YOU HAVE WHAT IT TAKES?

If you think you want to be your own boss and run your own business, but are not sure you have the right qualifications to be an entrepreneur, read on. What are the characteristics of an entrepreneur? How does an entrepreneur think? Is your personal profile similar to that of a successful entrepreneur?

Until recently, entrepreneurs were not widely studied. There was a general lack of knowledge and information about what made them tick. The recent interest in revitalizing America's dormant productivity has changed all that. Most business universities now offer courses in entrepreneurship. As a result, business professionals have learned a lot about what it takes to become a successful entrepreneur. Although no one has found the perfect entrepreneurial profile, there are many characteristics that show up repeatedly. In the sections that follow, we'll cover several important characteristics of entrepreneurs for you to consider and dispel the entrepreneurial myths.

ENTREPRENEURIAL CHARACTERISTICS

A series of interviews were conducted with distinguished entrepreneurs. They were asked what characteristics they felt were essential to success as an entrepreneur. Good health was a characteristic mentioned by every entrepreneur interviewed. Entrepreneurs are physically resilient and in good health. They can work for extended periods of time and, while they are in the process of building their business, they refuse to get sick.

In small businesses, where there is no depth of management, the leader must be there. You may not be able to afford a support staff to cover all business functions, and therefore you will need to work long hours. We all know people who use part of their sick leave each year when they are not sick. Entrepreneurs are not found in this group. At the end of the eight-hour day, when everyone else leaves for home, the entrepreneur will often continue to work into the evening, developing new business ideas.

Self-control

Entrepreneurs do not function well in structured organisations and do not like someone having authority over them. Most believe they can do the job better than anyone else and will strive for maximum responsibility and accountability. They enjoy creating business strategies and thrive on the process of achieving their goals. Once they achieve a goal, they quickly replace it with a greater goal. They strive to exert whatever influence they can over future events.

In large, structured organisations, entrepreneurs are easy to recognise by the statements they make: 'If they wanted that job done right, they should have given it to me.' A dominant characteristic of entrepreneurs is their belief that they are smarter than their peers and superiors. They have a compelling need to do their own thing in their own way. They need the freedom to choose and to act according to their own perception of what actions will result in success.

Self-confidence

Entrepreneurs are self-confident when they are in control of what they're doing and working alone. They tackle problems immediately with confidence and are persistent in their pursuit of their objectives. Most are at their best in the face of adversity, since they thrive on their own self-confidence.

Sense of urgency

Entrepreneurs have a never-ending sense of urgency to develop their ideas. Inactivity makes them impatient, tense and uneasy. They thrive on activity and are not likely to be found sitting on a bank fishing unless the fish are biting. When they are in the entrepreneurial mode, they are more likely to be found getting things done instead of fishing.

Entrepreneurs prefer individual sports, such as golf, skiing or tennis, over team sports. They prefer games in which their own brawn and brain directly influence the outcome and pace of the game. They have drive and high energy levels, they are achievement-oriented, and they are tireless in the pursuit of their goals.

Comprehensive awareness

Successful entrepreneurs can comprehend complex situations that may include planning, making strategic decisions, and working on multiple business ideas simultaneously. They are far-sighted and aware of important details, and they will continuously review all possibilities to achieve their business objectives. At the same time, they devote their energy to completing the tasks immediately before them.

Accounting reports illustrate this characteristic. Accountants spend hours balancing the accounts and closing them out. For them the achievement is to have balanced books. The entrepreneur only wants to know the magnitude of the numbers and their significance for the operation of the business.

Realism

Entrepreneurs accept things as they are and deal with them accordingly. They may or may not be idealistic, but they are seldom unrealistic. They will change their direction when they see that change will improve their prospects for achieving their goals. They want to know the status of a given situation at all times. News interests them if it is timely, and factual, and provides them with information they need. They will verify the information they receive before they use it in making a decision. Entrepreneurs say what they mean and assume that everyone else does too. They tend to be too trusting and may not be sufficiently suspicious in their business dealings with other people.

Conceptual ability

Entrepreneurs possess the ability to identify relationships quickly in the midst of complex situations. They identify problems and begin working on their solution faster than other people. They are not troubled by ambiguity and uncertainty because they are used to solving problems. Entrepreneurs are natural leaders and are usually the first to identify a problem to be overcome. If it is pointed out to them that their solution to a problem will not work for some valid reason, they will quickly identify an alternative problem-solving approach.

Status requirements

Entrepreneurs find satisfaction in symbols of success that are external to themselves. They like the business they have built to be praised, but they are often embarrassed by praise directed at them personally. Their egos do not prevent them from seeking facts, data and guidance. When they need help, they will not hesitate to admit it especially in areas that are outside of their expertise. During tough business periods, entrepreneurs will concentrate their resources and energies on essential business operations. They want to be where the action is and will not stay in the office for extended periods of time.

Symbols of achievement such as position have little relevance to them. Successful entrepreneurs find their satisfaction of status needs in the performance of their business, not in the appearance they present to their peers and to the public. They will postpone acquiring status items like a luxury car until they are certain that their business is stable.

Interpersonal relationships

Entrepreneurs are more concerned with people's accomplishments than with their feelings. They generally avoid becoming personally involved and will not hesitate to sever relationships that could hinder the progress of their business. During the business-building period, when resources are scarce, they seldom devote time to dealing with satisfying people's feelings beyond what is essential to achieving their goals.

Their lack of sensitivity to people's feelings can cause turmoil and turnover in their organisation. Entrepreneurs are impatient and drive themselves and everyone around them. They don't have the tolerance or empathy necessary for team building unless it's their team, and they will delegate very few key decisions.

As the business grows and assumes an organisational structure, entrepreneurs go through a classic management crisis. For many of them, their need for control makes it difficult for them to delegate authority in the way that a structured organisation demands. Their strong direct approach induces them to seek information directly from its source, bypassing the structured chains of authority and responsibility. Their moderate interpersonal skills, which were adequate during the start-up phases, will cause them problems as they try to adjust to the structured or corporate organisation. Entrepreneurs with good interpersonal skills will be able to adjust and survive as their organisation grows and becomes more structured. The rest won't make it.

Emotional stability

Entrepreneurs have a considerable amount of self-control and can handle business pressures. They are comfortable in stressful situations and are challenged rather than discouraged by setbacks or failures. Entrepreneurs are uncomfortable when things are going well. They'll frequently find some new activity on which to vent their pent-up energy. They are not content to leave well enough alone. Entrepreneurs tend to handle people problems with action plans without empathy. Their moderate interpersonal skills are often inadequate to provide for stable relationships. However, the divorce rate among entrepreneurs is about average.

B *Gerard International*

Values analysis for Company X

This exercise has been produced as an illustration of how values may be analysed in practice. It is the findings of a single return, is not statistically valid and does not necessarily represent Company X as they currently operate.

The information used in this exercise was produced wholly by Company X and neither Gerard International Ltd nor its servants or agents can be held responsible for any outcomes of Company X using this information in the management of their business.

SUMMARY

Company X have five recognised key values for their customer-facing business. In order of achievement in practice, these are:

- Value for money – 77 per cent
- Friendliness – 70 per cent
- Choice – 63 per cent
- Innovation – 60 per cent
- Quality – taken as perceived quality – 42 per cent.

INTRODUCTION

Gerard International Ltd, in working with a company called Strategic People, has developed a means of analysing 14 generic sets of values which are applicable to a business in terms of how they deliver business value to their customers as well as the values they display internally. The analysis uses both a questionnaire and a management game called *Dilemma!*

Adrian Davies of Gerard International has worked with Company X to deliver a publication which outlines their own five values and how the company has positively applied them to the management of their business. A preliminary match of Company X's values with Gerard's values is included as Figure B.1.

A manager of Company X kindly agreed to complete the questionnaire developed by Gerard International in order to explore how the key values for Company X may be analysed, mapped and prioritised.

In analysing the questionnaire, there are a number of assumptions:

- That the values relationship in Figure B.1 is correct. It was discussed in a meeting but not critically verified.
- That the questionnaire, as completed, relates specifically to the customer-focused aspects of the company – not internal values.

	Quality	Friendly	Innov'n	VFM	Choice	Overall	Internal
Sensitive		✓	✓	✓		✓	
Tough							✓
High trust	✓	✓		✓		✓	✓
Low trust							
Open		✓	✓	✓			
Closed							
Rational							✓
Emotional	✓	✓			✓		
Innovative			✓	✓		✓	
Traditional							?
Developmental			✓	✓		✓	✓
Opportunistic							
Image	✓	✓			✓	✓	
Outcomes							✓
People driven	✓	✓		✓		✓	
Systems driven							✓
Do now	✓	✓				✓	
Do later							✓
Thanking		✓			✓	✓	
Expecting							✓
Loyalty to others	✓			✓	✓	✓	✓
Loyalty to self							
Quality	✓		✓	✓	✓	✓	✓
Expediency							
Competitive							
Co-operative		✓		✓	✓	✓	✓
Hierarchical							✓
Informal		✓			✓	✓	

Figure B.1   Relationship grid between Company X and Gerard values

- That values need to be driven; and a mid-point (average) score for a pair of values is taken as a negative in this context.

Questionnaire analysis								
	Pref Value			Avge.			Pref Value	
Traditional				X				Innovative
Low trust					X			Trust
Emotional					X			Rational
Informal			X					Hierarchical
Image					X			Outcomes
Loyalty to others			X					Loyalty to self
Developmental			X					Opportunistic
People driven			X					Systems driven
Quality				X				Expediency
Do now				X				Do later
Closed						X		Open
Thanking		X						Expecting
Co-operative			X					Competitive
Tough					X			Sensitive

Figure B.2   The results of the analysis
The central column represents those responses from the questionnaire which analyse as neutral.
The preferred values for Company X are identified in the outer columns by shaded calls.

FINDINGS

The comparison of the questionnaire analysis and the preferred values is at Figure B.2. In looking at the values as practised and the preferred values it is taken that:

- For any value to be recognised or practised it should be a positive attribute, and those values which have analysed as neutral need to migrate to a definite preference.

    For example, the preferred value of traditional vs. innovative for Company X is innovative, yet the analysis provides a neutral outcome. To meet Company X's aspirations there needs to be a positive shift towards the customer focus becoming more innovative.

- Values on the same side of neutral as the preferred value need no further consideration.
- Values which are on the side of neutral away from the preferred value need to be addressed most positively.

OUTCOMES

- Nine sets of values as analysed are consistent with desired values for the business.
- Three sets of values need to be more positively developed and promoted, as they are perceived as neutral. These are:
  - to become more innovative;
  - to better address perceived quality; and
  - to have more of a 'do now' approach to customers.
- Two sets of values need to be significantly reviewed and, if appropriate, developmental programmes put in place to better deliver the desired service. These values are:
  - to become less rational and more emotional towards customers (difficult when there are lots of them needing to be quickly processed)
  - to be more concerned about the image the company delivers, compared with just doing the job as efficiently and safely as possible.

INFERENCES FOR COMPANY X

The outcomes from the questionnaire are compared with the five identified values, and summarised in Figure B.3; some of the five values more closely approach the ideal than others. A simple scoring of number of values which reach the ideal, compared with the number of values which comprise that ideal, gives the following levels of achievement:

- Value for money – 7 out of 9 (77 per cent)
- Friendliness – 7 out of 10 (70 per cent)
- Choice – 5 out of 8 (63 per cent)
- Innovation – 3 out of 5 (60 per cent)
- Quality – taken as perceived quality – 3 out of 7 (42 per cent).

RECOMMENDATIONS

That Company X explore more deeply their relationships with customers to get closer to them, their feelings and their perceptions of the company.

To be more aware of the image the company projects in a business which demands extreme efficiency to meet timetable, cost and safety standards.

REFLECTIONS

The closeness of the outcomes from this analysis to the desired values of the company is quite impressive and speaks well for the programmes in place.

	Quality	Friendly	Innov'n	VFM	Choice	Overall	Internal
Sensitive		✓	✓	✓		✓	
Tough							✓
High trust	✓	✓		✓		✓	✓
Low trust							
Open		✓	✓	✓		✓	✓
Closed							
Rational							✓
Emotional	✓	✓			✓	✓	
Innovative			✓	✓		✓	
Traditional							?
Developmental			✓	✓		✓	✓
Opportunistic							
Image	✓	✓			✓	✓	
Outcomes							✓
People driven	✓	✓		✓	✓	✓	
Systems driven							✓
Do now	✓	✓				✓	
Do later							✓
Thanking		✓			✓	✓	
Expecting							✓
Loyalty to others	✓			✓	✓	✓	✓
Loyalty to self							
Quality	✓		✓	✓	✓	✓	✓
Expediency							
Competitive							
Co-operative		✓		✓	✓	✓	✓
Hierarchical							✓
Informal		✓			✓	✓	
Score	3/7	7/10	3/5	7/9	5/8	9/14	
Closeness to ideal	42%	70%	60%	77%	63%	64%	

Figure B.3   The analysed elements scoring average (neutral) or in opposition to Company X's identified values

C *Johnson & Johnson*

Our Company

At Johnson & Johnson there is no mission statement that hangs on the wall. Instead, for more than 60 years, a simple, one-page document – Our Credo – has guided our actions in fulfilling our responsibilities to our customers, our employees, the community and our stockholders. Our worldwide Family of Companies shares this value system in 36 languages spreading across Africa, Asia/Pacific, Eastern Europe, Europe, Latin America, Middle East and North America.

OUR CREDO

We believe our first responsibility is to the doctors, nurses and to patients, to mothers and fathers and all others who use our products and services. In meeting their needs everything we do must be of high quality. We must constantly strive to reduce our costs in order to maintain reasonable prices. Customers' orders must be serviced promptly and accurately. Our suppliers and distributors must have an opportunity to make a fair profit.

We are responsible to our employees, the men and women who work with us throughout the world. Everyone must be considered as an individual. We must respect their dignity and recognize their merit. They must have a sense of security in their jobs. Compensation must be fair and adequate, and working conditions clean, orderly and safe. We must be mindful of ways to help our employees fulfil their family responsibilities. Employees must feel free to make suggestions and complaints. There must be equal opportunity for employment, development and advancement for those qualified. We must provide competent management, and their actions must be just and ethical.

We are responsible to the communities in which we live and work and to the world community as well. We must be good citizens – support good works and charities and bear our fair share of taxes. We must encourage civic improvements and better health and education. We must maintain in good order the property we are privileged to use, protecting the environment and natural resources.

Our final responsibility is to our stockholders. Business must make a sound profit. We must experiment with new ideas. Research must be carried on, innovative programs developed and mistakes paid for. New equipment must be purchased, new facilities provided and new products launched. Reserves must be created to provide for adverse times. When we operate according to these principles, the stockholders should realize a fair return.

D The SPL Corporate Health Check*

Recent events underline the need to maintain shareholder and public confidence in companies. Confidence, however, has to have a basis in reality. While it is likely that shareholders and other stakeholders may perceive the company to be well-managed, the chairperson and directors need to be reassured that this perception is well founded.

The Strategic Partnership (London) Limited (SPL), a leading strategic consulting firm specialising in stakeholder strategy and enterprise risk management, has developed a 'corporate health check', a process akin to the concept of a health check individuals undergo as a means of monitoring their well-being and identifying incipient risks.

What is the SPL Corporate Health Check?

The SPL Corporate Health Check provides a quick, but thorough, diagnosis of the health of the company. It is designed to provide the board, through a professional, independent and objective review, with the assurance that it is properly exercising and fulfilling its responsibilities and that there are no submerged issues which could affect the integrity, health, sustainability or reputation of the company. Its diagnostic process differs from others by focussing on the future in order to prioritise action to address present concerns.

All organisations have a diverse mix of assets, both tangible and intangible, which, if managed in a strategic and long-term manner, will open up new areas of sustainable business and profit. While all organisations are different and no simple formula will fit all circumstances, the board's processes and systems will need to be supported by seven intangible attributes that require investment and maintenance in order to sustain current and future business prospects and net financial result. These are:

- a vision into the future
- leadership and effective internal communication
- clearly defined culture, values and behaviours
- knowledge, skills and competencies
- earned reputation and trust
- engagement with stakeholders
- managed relationships and communication with the wider community.

---

* © Peter Smith. Reproduced with kind permission.

KEY ISSUES ADDRESSED BY THE SPL CORPORATE HEALTH CHECK

In addition to the assessment of the seven intangible attributes, other key issues integral to the effectiveness of a company's management are addressed during the course of a Corporate Health Check:

Intangible assets
- Strategies
- Capabilities
- Stakeholder contribution
- Processes
- Stakeholder satisfaction
- Licence to operate.

Governance
- Board structure and balance
- The chairperson's role and responsibilities
- Directors' responsibilities generally (including conflicts of interest)
- The company secretary and management of the board
- Board delegation and reporting by management
- Implementation of board strategy and decisions
- Measurement of performance
- Assessment of risk to the business and internal control
- Corporate policies and codes of business practice
- Board committees – Audit, Remuneration and Nomination
- Directors' service contracts and other arrangements, including transactions.

External driving factors
- Relevant legislation and other anticipated statutory interventions
- The impact of politically generated imperatives
- Changing demands from regulators and reporting regimes
- Response to incidents which may impact negatively on reputation
- Response to economic pressures and investor attitudes
- Issues of diversity, equal opportunities and racial equality
- Response to public and media attitudes
- Communities and the environment.

METHODOLOGY

Through a diagnostic and self-assessment process, we start by defining an organisation's key stakeholder dynamics and go on to develop an objective analysis of the board's effectiveness in managing these dynamics and the interaction between them.

The Health Check process involves a series of workshops and confidential interviews, first with the board and senior management and then with agreed representative groups of institutional and private shareholders, customers, suppliers, employees and the wider community. The workshops and interviews are used to agree what 'good' looks like in each of the identified key dynamics and to compare how the company sees itself with the interaction of stakeholder views and expectations of the company. This comparison is made against two sets of questions.

Future activities
- What is changing in the external world?
- How does this affect where we want to go?
- How do we invest for the future?

The focus here is on building options and flexibility for the future, understanding how the business context is likely to change and what needs to be done to drive or, at least, take advantage of change.

Current activities
- Where are we now?
- What do we need to change?
- What action should we take?

The focus here is on reviewing what the organisation does and reflecting on where improvements might be achieved in ways to increase value.

DELIVERABLES

On completion of the diagnostic process, the Corporate Health Check will have identified existing practices where improvements are required and aspects of the corporate well-being that may need further attention in order to sustain its future. These results are then presented to the board in an interactive workshop, facilitated by SPL, at which priorities for attention are identified, a plan for dealing with them is outlined and responsibilities for action are agreed.

The Corporate Health Check is undertaken by a small team of SPL's highly experienced consultants, assisted, as appropriate, by personnel drawn from partner organisations. The Health Check normally takes between eight and ten weeks to complete and the findings are available within two weeks of the diagnostic process being completed. However, if a Health Check is required to concentrate on a particular aspect of a company's affairs, the time required will be adjusted accordingly.

TESTIMONIALS IN SUPPORT OF THE SPL CORPORATE HEALTH CHECK

The SPL Corporate Health Check has been endorsed by the following:

There couldn't be a better time to promote the concept of a health check for companies as a means of monitoring their well-being and identifying incipient risks in the way they manage their intangible assets. The 'softer' areas of business are attracting increasing focus and importance for ensuring survival, sustainability and long-term shareholder value. With boards appearing to be increasingly uncertain about whether they really understand the businesses and risks for which they are responsible, SPL's initiative in providing a comprehensive, forward-looking and independent enterprise risk assessment of corporate health is one which I strongly commend companies to undertake.

Sir Digby Jones, Director-General, Confederation of British Industry

SPL's Corporate Health Check is a welcome initiative and one which companies would be wise to undertake.

Chris Hirst, Chief Investment Manager, Cooperative Insurance Society

As a leading representative of major institutional shareholders, the NAPF welcomes the concept of a health check for companies, whereby management may obtain in independent appraisal of its corporate process when facing the challenges ahead. The SPL Corporate Health Check, which focuses on intangible issues, should provide a valuable contribution to this area.

David Gould, Director of Investment, National Association of Pension Funds

The Corporate Health Check supports the levels of best practice in the area of risk management which we expect companies to achieve.

Peter Butler, Chief Executive, Hermes Focus Investment Management

The Corporate Health Check goes beyond mere box-ticking into the crucial areas which corporate governance should always – but too often does not – address.

Philip Goldenberg, a Corporate Finance Partner in City Solicitors, S.J. Berwin, and Advisor to the Company Law Review about directors, shareholders and stakeholders

We welcome this Health Check initiative by SPL as a means of helping companies achieve high standards of governance.

Ken Rushton, Head of the UK Listing Authority, Financial Services Authority

I was interested to read the approach which you at SPL have adopted and you have clearly set out the key issues which need to be addressed. There could be no more appropriate time for boards to accept your offer of a Corporate Health Check. What impressed me most about your document was, first, the accent on looking ahead to preparing for future challenges rather than simply dealing with the past and present and, second, the calibre of the team which SPL is fielding.

Sir Adrian Cadbury

Bibliography

The following books and articles are recommended for further reading. Many are referred to, and quoted, in the text of *The Practice of Corporate Governance*.

Reports and codes

Cadbury Report (and Code) (Gee, 1992).
Greenbury Report (and Code) (Gee, 1995).
Hampel Report (and Combined Code) (Gee, 1998).
Higgs Report (2003).
Nolan Report (1995).
Smith Report (2003).
Tomorrow's Company (RSA, 1995).
Turnbull Report (ICA, 1999).
Combined Code (2003).

General

A Strategic Approach to Corporate Governance, Adrian Davies (Gower, 1999).
Corporate Governance, Kevin Keasey and Mike Wright (Wiley, 1997).
Corporate Governance, Ira M. Millstein et al. (OECD, 1998).
Corporate Governance, Robert A.G. Monks and Nell Minow (Blackwell, 1995).
Corporate Governance: A Director's Guide (IOD, 2004).
Corporate Governance: A Framework for Implementation, Magdi R. Iskander and Nadereh Chamlon (World Bank, 2000).
Corporate Governance: The New Strategic Imperative (EIU, 2002).
Family Firms and their Governance, Sir Adrian Cadbury (Egon Zehnder International, 2000).
Having their Cake…: How the City and Big Bosses are Consuming UK Business, Don Young and Pat Scott (Kogan Page, 2004).
Hidden Champions, Hermann Simon (Harvard Business School Press, 1996).
The Future at the Bottom of the Pyramid: Eradicating Poverty through Profits, C.K. Pralahad (Wharton School, 2004).
The Handbook of International Corporate Governance (IoD, 2004).
The Iron Triangle, Dan Briody (Wiley, 2003).
The Strategic Role of Marketing, Adrian Davies (McGraw Hill, 1995).
Watching the Watchers: Corporate Governance for the 21st Century, Robert A.G. Monks and Nell Minow (Blackwell, 1996).

Boards

Anchoring Points for Corporate Directors: Enforcing the Unenforceable, Robert K. Mueller (Quorum Books, 1996).
Corporate Boards that Create Value, John Carver and Caroline Oliver, (Jossey-Bass, 2004).
Corporate Governance and Chairmanship, Sir Adrian Cadbury (Oxford University Press, 2002).
'Leadership Board of Directors', Adrian Davies, Paul Joyce, Graham Beaver and Adrian Woods, *Strategic Change* (June/July, 2002).
Saving the Corporate Board, Ralph D. Ward (Wiley, 2003).
Thin on Top, Bob Garratt (Nicholas Brealey, 2003).

Leadership

Bad Leadership, Barbara Kellerman (Harvard Business School, 2004).
Contests for Corporate Control, Mary A. O'Sullivan (Oxford University Press, 2000).
Enterprise, Roger Parry (Profile Books, 2003).
Focus on Leadership, Larry Spears and Michele Lawrence (Wiley, 2002).
'Great Companies to Work For' (*Fortune*, 2 February 2004).
Hardball, G. Stalk and R. Lachenauer (Harvard Business School, 2004).
How to Run a Company, D. Carey and M.C. Von Weichs (Crown Business, 2003).
Rewiring the Corporate Brain, Danah Zohar (Berret-Koehler, 1997).
The Allure of Toxic Leaders, Jean Lipman-Blumen (Oxford University Press, 2004).
The Engaging Leader, Ed Gubman (Dearborn, 2003).
The Fish Rots from the Head, Bob Garratt (Harper Collins, 1996).
The Leader's Voice, Boyd Clarke and Ron Crossland (Select Books, 2002).
The Right CEO, Frederick W. Wacherle (Jossey-Bass, 2001).
'Understanding Entrepreneurship', Jonathan Guthrie (*Financial Times*, 12 November 2003).

Accountability

Corporate Governance: Accountability in the Market Place (attacks stakeholder accountability), Elaine Sternberg (IEA, 1998, 2004).
Corporate Governance: An Action Plan for Profitability, Thomas Sheridan and Nigel Kendall (Pitman, 1992).
Institutional Shareholders and Corporate Governance, G.P. Stapledon (Clarendon Press, 1996).
'Look Beyond the Details of Higgs', Richard Lapthorne (*Financial Times*, 24 November 2004).
Morality and the Market (social control of business), N. Graig Smith (Routledge, 1990).
Private Business – Public Battleground, John Egan and Des Wilson (Palgrave, 2002).
The Company of Strangers, Paul Seabright (Princeton, 2004).
'The Perils of CSR', Stefan Stern, *RSA Journal* (January, 2004).
'The Reputation Quotient', C.J. Fombrun, N.A. Gardberg and J.M. Sever (*Journal of Brand Management*, 2000).

Index